THE RULE OF THE SECULAR FRANCISCAN ORDER

with a Catechism and Instructions

THE RULE OF THE SECULAR FRANCISCAN ORDER

WITH A CATECHISM AND INSTRUCTIONS

Catechism by
Fr. Conelio Mota Ramos O.F.M.
and translated by
Fr. Felipe Baldonado O.F.M.

Instructions compiled by
Capuchin Friars and Secular Franciscans
of the Province of St. Mary
and edited by
Fr. Zachary Grant O.F.M. Cap.

Franciscan Press
Quincy University
1800 College Avenue
Quincy, Illinois 62301-2699
Telephone: 217-228-5670 • FAX: 217-228-5672

The Rule of the Secular Franciscan Order, with a Catechism and Instructions. Catechism, by Fr. Cornelio Mota Ramos O.F.M. and translated by Fr. Felipe Baldonado O.F.M.; *Instructions,* compiled by Capuchin Friars and Secular Franciscans of the Province of St. Mary and edited by Fr. Zachary Grant O.F.M. Cap.

Library of Congress Cataloging in Publication Data:
Main entry under title:

The Rule of the Secular Franciscan Order

1. Franciscans. Third Order–Rules
I. Ramos, Cornelio Mota. II. Grant, Zachary.

B X3654.A3R84 1981 255′.3 80-20635

Published with Ecclesiastical Permission

MADE IN THE UNITED STATES OF AMERICA

FOREWORD

To provide Secular Franciscans of the English-speaking world with a manual containing not only the text but also an explanation of their new rule, we have assembled in one handy volume:

(1) the approval of the rule by Pope John Paul II and other documents which introduced the new rule;

(2) the approved English translation of the rule with a short official commentary in parallel columns;

(3) a catechism which succinctly analyzes and explains the rule in question and answer form;

(4) two series of instructions on the rule, namely six instructions for postulants before their initiation as Secular Franciscans and twelve instructions for novices before their profession of the rule.

The eighteen instructions (Part IV), inasmuch as they are an exposition of the new rule, are suitable also for reading and study by professed members of the Secular Franciscan Order who feel the need of a better understanding of the rule. They will also supply material and suggestions to the spiritual assistants for conferences on the rule.

Another exposition of the new rule of the Secular Franciscan Order is contained in the articles which have appeared in the monthly magazine *Franciscan Herald,* "official organ of the National Fraternity of the Secular Franciscan Order" (U.S.A.), volumes LVIII (1979) and LIX (1980), especially the serialized "common reflection prepared by the national assistants' commission for commentary on the new rule." *Tolle et lege!* Take and read!

— The Editor.

CONTENTS

PART I

DOCUMENTS

1. DECREE OF PROMULGATION

THE RULE OF THE SECULAR FRANCISCAN ORDER IS APPROVED AND CONFIRMED — Pope Paul VI

In perpetual remembrance. — The Seraphic Patriarch St. Francis of Assisi, during his life and even after his beautiful death, not only attracted many to serve God in the religious family founded by him, but also drew numerous members of the laity to enter his communities while remaining in the world (as far as possible). Moreover, to use the words of our predecessor Pius XI, "it seems . . . that there was never anyone in whom there shone forth more vividly and who resembled more the image of Jesus Christ and the evangelic form of life than Francis. Accordingly, he who was called the *Herald of the Great King* was rightly hailed as *another Christ* for he presented himself to his contemporaries and to future ages as Christ returned to life. Consequently, he still lives as such in the eyes of men and will continue to live for all ages to come." (Encyc. "Rite Expiatis," April 30, 1926: AAS, 18, 1926, p. 154.)

We are happy that the "Franciscan charism" today is still a force for the good of the Church and the human community, despite the infiltration of doctrines and tendencies that alienate people from God and from the supernatural.

With praiseworthy initiative and with common accord the four Franciscan families for ten years have striven to prepare a new rule for the Franciscan Third Order Secular, or as it is now called, the Secular Franciscan Order. This was necessary because of the changed conditions of the times and because of the teaching and encouragement given them by the Second Vatican Council. Therefore, our dearly beloved Sons, the four ministers general of the Franciscan Order, have requested that we approve the Rule presented to us. Following the example of some of our predecessors, the latest being Pope Leo XIII, we have willingly decided to grant their request. In this way, we nurture the hope that the form of life preached by that admirable man of Assisi will gain a new impetus and will flourish vigorously.

Having consulted with the Sacred Congregation for Religious and Secular Institutes, which has diligently examined and carefully evaluated the text, we approve and confirm with our apostolic authority and sanction the *Rule of the Secular Franciscan Order,* provided that it agrees with the copy in the archives of the Sacred Congregation for Religious and Secular Institutes, beginning with the words, "The Franciscan family," and ending with "according to the norm of the constitutions." By this letter and our apostolic authority, we abrogate the previous rule of what was formerly called the Franciscan Third Order. Finally, we decree that this letter remains in effect now and in the future, regardless of anything contrary.

Given at Rome at St. Peter's, under the ring of the Fisherman, on June 24, 1978, the 16th year of our pontificate.

John Cardinal Villot
Secretary of State

2. LETTER OF THE FOUR MINISTERS GENERAL OF THE FRANCISCAN FAMILY

To the Brothers and Sisters of the Secular Franciscan Order on the occasion of granting the Rule approved by the Holy See:

We joyfully inform you that the Holy See, by means of

the Apostolic Letter *Seraphicus Patriarca,* dated June 24, 1978, and "under the ring of the Fisherman," has approved the revised *Rule of the Secular Franciscan Order* which abrogates and takes the place of the preceding rule of Pope Leo XIII.

It is to Pope Paul VI that we owe this splendid gift, which he bestowed shortly before he left this earth. He loved you. Many times, indeed, he demonstrated his love for the Secular Franciscan Order and addressed to you unforgettable words, as in June of 1968 and in 1971 on the occasion of the 750th anniversary of *Memoriale Propositi.*

Since March 7, 1966, when the Sacred Congregation for Religious granted permission to begin updating legislation for the Secular Franciscan Order, the journey has been long and arduous.

We wish to underscore the work accomplished by the brothers and sisters and by the fraternities through the National Councils, through such publications as *Way of Life* and *Journeys,* and by the tireless work of the Presidency of the International Council since its establishment in 1973.

Such work was of primary importance in seeking the ways of the spirit and most efficacious in recognizing the presence and the vitality of the Franciscan charism in the People of God in our day.

The rule that we present to you today is not only the fruit of [much] labor. The Church consigns it to you as a norm of life.

Notice first its evangelical content; welcome the Franciscan message that it contains and the guidance it offers you in living according to the holy gospel.

The hope of renewal hinges upon returning to the origins and to the spiritual experience of Francis of Assisi and of the brothers and sisters of penance who received from him their inspiration and guidance. This sentiment is also included in the prologue, "Letter to the Faithful" (recensio prior) and in the constant references to the teaching and example of St. Francis. This renewal also depends upon openness to the Spirit in the signs of the times.

Supported by this foundation, you should put into practice the invitation of the rule to be creative and to exercise coresponsibility.

This creativity, in certain cases, should express itself in the form of statutes. Indeed, number 3 of the rule states as a general norm: "Its application will be made by the General Constitutions and particular statutes."

We, the Franciscan Ministers, with all our friars are ever ready and open to offer you all our assistance so that we may walk together in the way of the Lord.

With these sentiments we are pleased to present the revised *Rule of the Secular Franciscan Order* to the Presidency of the International Council and through this Council to all Secular Franciscans who will receive it as a norm of life.

Rome, October 4, 1978

Fr. Constantine Koser O.F.M.
Fr. Vitale M. Bommarco O.F.M.Conv.
Fr. Paschal Rywalski O.F.M.Cap.
Fr. Roland J. Faley T.O.R.

3. LETTER OF THE INTERNATIONAL PRESIDENT

October 4, 1978

Dear Brothers and Sisters,

The ten year wait for the new rule has finally had a favorable outcome. On October 4th, feast of our Seraphic Father St. Francis, the Ministers General of the Franciscan Order passed down to the Presidency of the International Council, Franciscan Third Order, the new rule which was approved on June 24, 1978, by the late Pontiff, Paul VI. I consider it a supreme gift from this Pope who was a true Franciscan in his heart and in his works.

We ask all the National Councils to promote in their

respective regions, provinces, and individual fraternities the knowledge of the new rule and encourage its study, so that it may be appreciated and understood in accord with the mind of St. Francis as "the marrow of the gospel, the way of perfection" (cf. II Celano, 208).

With the promulgation of the new rule, renewal of the Secular Fraternity has reached a decisive and powerful moment, but is not yet completed. We must still arrange for the renewal of the Constitutions and Statutes. And, in fulfilling the work of post-conciliar *aggiornamento,* it is necessary that they be clearly rooted in the spirit of the Secular Franciscan Order as set forth in the new rule.

We thank the Fathers General for having delivered this rule over to us, and we beg all the brothers and sisters to cherish it, to know it well, but above all to live it daily so they will be able "to die with it" (cf. II Celano, 208).

Manuela Mattioli

4. MESSAGE FROM HUMBERTO CARDINAL MEDEIROS

Liaison between the American Bishops and the National Fraternity of the Secular Franciscan Order - U.S.A.

December 27, 1978

May the Lord give you his Peace!

St. Francis of Assisi brought to the Church of the 13th century a new and profound understanding of what it meant to "live the gospel." His spirit is embodied in the three Orders which make up the Franciscan Family, and has been given a dimension for our own times with the approval by Pope Paul VI of a new rule for the Secular Franciscan Order.

We rejoice with the whole Church in great expectation as the Order is given new vitality. This rule not only places the Secular Order squarely within the post-conciliar renewal, but returns Franciscans to their origins as a movement of penance among the people of God.

Looking to the person of Jesus, sent by his Father to live among us, Franciscans see a life of penance as nothing less than one which in simplicity and joy imitates the poverty, suffering, and humble service to his people which characterized the earthly life of the Son of God as revealed in the gospel.

Secular Franciscans are now called to re-study the gospel as their first rule, so their lives will show forth the total surrender of Jesus to the will of his Father. The new rule does not spell out *how* to do this, but rather *why*. Yet, responding to your love-filled awareness that the Son of God shared our human condition as a brother, you will live in a way that reflects that belief with the abandon that moved St. Francis.

Your example is particularly needed within our own country, and can greatly help "to build up the Body of Christ" here in the United States. The simplicity of your life-style will show forth the poverty of Christ so as to combat the materialism which engulfs us. Your identification with his cross, that act of total self-surrender, will make you our defense against the sensuality of this age, a hedonism which is undermining the foundation of family life and the sacredness of human love. And in letting yourselves "be imposed upon in joyful service" to your brothers and sisters who are in need, you will demonstrate the gospel meaning of self-fulfillment, which demands that we work at respecting the dignity of all God's people, especially the poor and the victims of social and economic prejudice.

Thus we in the United States of America need Secular Franciscans to be our constant reminder that we are the Church of the poor and crucified Savior, Jesus Christ, who "did not come to be served, but to serve and to give his life for the ransom of many."

The new rule leaves no doubt that the purpose of the Secular Franciscan Order is to live "in full communion with the pope, bishops, and priests" in order to bring about a "rebuilding of the Church." You are to be instruments of peace in the Church and in the world, and to promote justice among all peoples so that the Kingdom of God can advance towards its full realization. Because as laity you have an intimate involvement in social, economic, and cultural affairs, as Secular Franciscans you must be ready to use your time and talents in all these areas to bring the Church's mission to them which is the voice of Christ. This should be especially evident within the sphere of the local parish community.

Therefore, in all sincerity and humility as your Cardinal, I call on all Secular Franciscans, and particularly the leaders of the Order, to rise to the challenge of your new rule. The Church has much to lose if you fail to survive the call of the bishops for renewal. And you must not wait for others to lead you. The Church expects you as mature Christians to strike out boldly and in all simplicity and trust to bring to us all the apostolic spirit of St. Francis. Thus you will not only be a true penitential movement, but be carrying out the proper role of the laity among the People of God as taught by the II Vatican Council.

You need have no fear that it can be done. In your Secular Franciscan vocation you are guided by Mary, the Mother of Jesus, under whose protection you were placed by St. Francis. United in prayer with her as the Mother of the Church, and with all her children through the Eucharist may the followers of the Little Poor Man of Assisi fulfill their service to Jesus, who is the gift of love from our heavenly Father.

PART II

THE RULE

Text

RULE OF THE SECULAR FRANCISCAN ORDER

Prologue: Exhortation of Saint Francis to the Brothers and Sisters in Penance.

In the name of the Lord!

Chapter One

Concerning Those Who Do Penance

All who love the Lord with their whole heart, with their whole soul and mind, with all their strength (cf. Mk 12:30), and love their neighbors as themselves (cf. Mt 22: 39) and hate their bodies with their vices and sins, and receive the Body and Blood of our Lord Jesus Christ, and produce worthy fruits of penance:

Oh, how happy and blessed are these men and women when they do these things and persevere in doing them, because "the spirit of the Lord will rest upon them" (cf. Is 11:2) and he will make "his home and dwelling among them" (cf. Jn 14:23), and they are the sons of the heavenly Father (cf. Mt 5:45), whose works they do, and they are the spouses, brothers, and mothers of our Lord Jesus Christ (cf. Mt 12:50).

We are spouses, when by the Holy Spirit the faithful soul is united with our Lord Jesus Christ, we are brothers to him when we fulfill "the will of the Father who is in heaven" (Mt 12:50).

We are mothers, when we carry him in our heart and body (cf. 1 Cor 6:20) through divine love and a pure and sincere conscience; we give birth to him through a holy life which must give light to others by example (cf. Mt 5:16).

Commentary

OFFICIAL COMMENTARY

Prologue

1.

The new rule is prefaced by a word from St. Francis himself. This text, a new version of the "Letter to All the Faithful," is both a summary of Franciscan gospel living and an immediate contact with the model and inspiration for observing the gospel — Francis himself.

Francis' letter touches two points: the life of a person who does "penance" (i.e., a person turned toward God), and the life of a person who refuses this grace.

First of all, a person turned toward God follows the "teaching and footsteps of our Lord Jesus Christ" by responding to the inviting grace of God and living in union with Jesus: constant spiritual renewal, awareness of God's power and presence, and a promise of eternal happiness. Most appropriate are the quotes from Jesus' high priestly prayer which make the intense union between Jesus and his disciples and their union among themselves the model for our own union with Christ and with others. Francis bids us to live the gospel of Jesus Christ by loving the Lord our God and serving our neighbor, by participating in the holy Eucharist and thereby building a lived experience of togetherness, by rejecting sin and turning in a new direction, and

Text

Oh, how glorious it is to have a great and holy Father in heaven! oh how glorious it is to have such a beautiful and admirable Spouse, the Holy Paraclete!

Oh, how glorious it is to have such a Brother and such a Son, loved, beloved, humble, peaceful, sweet, lovable, and desirable above all: Our Lord Jesus Christ, who gave up his life for his sheep (cf. Jn 10:15) and prayed to the Father saying:

"O holy Father, protect them with your name (cf. Jn 17:11) whom you gave me out of the world. I entrusted to them the message you entrusted to me and they received it. They have known that in truth I came from you, they have believed that it was you who sent me. For these I pray, not for the world (cf. Jn 17:9). Bless and consecrate them, and I consecrate myself for their sakes. I do not pray for them alone; I pray also for those who will believe in me through their word (cf. Jn 17:20) that they may be holy by being one as we are (cf. Jn 17:11). And I desire, Father, to have them in my company where I am to see this glory of mine in your kingdom" (cf. Jn 17:6-24).

Commentary

by leading a life in which we mirror Christ. This leads to a new kind of happiness, for we share the Lord's life and mission and we give him birth again and again in our world. This summary of gospel living in the prologue prefigures the second chapter of the rule.

Chapter Two

Concerning Those Who Do Not Do Penance

But all those men and women who are not doing penance and do not receive the Body and Blood of our Lord Jesus Christ and live in vices and sin and yield to evil concupiscence and to the wicked desires of the flesh, and do not observe what they have promised to the Lord, and are slaves to the world, in their bodies, by carnal desires and the anxieties and cares of this life (cf. Jn 8:41):

These are blind, because they do not see the true light, our Lord Jesus Christ; they

2.

Secondly, the person who refuses this grace lacks wisdom and light, loses one's perspective on striving for perfect joy, and finds oneself enslaved and smothered by the demonic influences of life. Hence, no happiness in this world or the next. Francis' words are stark, straightforward and uncompromising, but the core message is valid and ever-true.

do not have spiritual wisdom because they do not have the Son of God who is the true wisdom of the Father. Concerning them, it is said, "Their skill was swallowed up" (Ps 107:27) and "cursed are those who turn away from your commands" (Ps 119:21). They see and acknowledge, they know and do bad things and knowingly destroy their own souls.

See, you who are blind, deceived by your enemies, the world, the flesh and the devil, for it is pleasant to the body to commit sin and it is bitter to make it serve God because all vices and sins come out and "proceed from the heart of man" as the Lord says in the gospel (cf. Mt 7:21). And you have nothing in this world and in the next, and you thought you would possess the vanities of this world for a long time.

But you have been deceived, for the day and the hour will come to which you give no thought and which you do not know and of which you are ignorant. The body grows infirm, death approaches, and so it dies a bitter death, and no matter where or when or how man dies, in the guilt of sin, without penance or satisfaction, though he can make satisfaction but does not do it.

The devil snatches the soul from his body with such anguish and tribulation that no one can know it except he who endures it, and all the talents and power and "knowledge and wisdom" (2 Chr 1:17) which they thought they had will be taken away from them (cf. Lk 8:18; Mk 4:25), and they leave their goods to relatives and friends who take and divide them and say afterwards, "Cursed be his soul because he could have given us more, he could have acquired more than he did." The worms eat up the body and so they have lost body and soul during this short earthly life and will go into the inferno where they will suffer torture without end.

All those into whose hands this letter shall have come we ask in the charity that is God (cf. 1 Jn 4:17) to accept kindly and with divine love the fragrant words of our Lord Jesus Christ quoted above. And let those who do not know how to read have them read to them.

And may they keep them in their mind and carry them out, in a holy manner to the end, because they are "spirit and life" (Jn 6:64).

And those who will not do this will have to render "an account on the day of judgment" (cf. Mt 12:36) before the tribunal of our Lord Jesus Christ (cf. Rom 14:10).

(Cajetan Esser O.F.M., *Die Opuscula des hl. Franziskus von Assisi.* Nuova Ediz. Critica, Grottaferrata, 1976; translated by Marion A. Habig O.F.M.)

Rule of the Secular Franciscan Order

Text

Chapter One
The Secular Franciscan Order (S.F.O.) [1]

1.

The Franciscan family, as one among many spiritual families raised up by the Holy Spirit in the Church,[2] unites all members of the people of God — laity, religious, and priests — who recognize that they are called to follow Christ in the footsteps of Saint Francis of Assisi.[3]

In various ways and forms but in life-giving union with each other, they intend to make present the charism of their common Seraphic Father in the life and mission of the Church.[4]

2.

The Secular Franciscan Order holds a special place in this family circle. It is an organic union of all Catholic fraternities scattered throughout the world and open to every group of the faithful. In these fraternities the brothers and sisters, led by the Spirit, strive for perfect charity in their own secular state. By their profession they pledge themselves to live the gospel in the manner of Saint Francis by means of this rule approved by the Church.[5]

3.

The present rule, succeeding "Memoriale Propositi" (1221) and the rules approved by the Supreme Pontiffs Nicholas IV and Leo XIII, adapts the Secular Franciscan Order to the needs and expectations of the Holy Church in the conditions of changing times. Its interpretation belongs to the Holy See and its application will be made by the General Constitutions and particular statutes.

Commentary

Chapter One
Secular Franciscan Order

1.

This first chapter details the place of the Secular Franciscan Order in the Church, in the Franciscan Family, and in the history of the Order itself.

The first paragraph shows how the Franciscan Family, as one of the many spiritual families in the Church, is united with all the people of God by the call of the Holy Spirit and the following of Jesus Christ. Still, in addition to this, the way of Francis gives the Franciscan Family, with its common charism but varied expressions, a distinctive cast, as it strives for holiness and binds together the laity, religious and clergy in the life and mission of the Church.

2.

This second paragraph identifies the Secular Franciscan Order as a vital part of the whole family of Francis and points out its special secular character. It also stresses that all the necessary prerequisites are present to make it an official Order within the Catholic Church.

3.

The continuity with past rules, its influence in today's world, and its approval by the Church are discussed in this third paragraph. This rule is the fourth expression in eight centuries. It makes the unchanging principles of Franciscan gospel living applicable and relevant today. The leaders of the Church constantly guide this movement from gospel to life.

Text

Chapter Two
The Way of Life

4.

The rule and life of the Secular Franciscans is this: to observe the gospel of our Lord Jesus Christ by following the example of Saint Francis of Assisi, who made Christ the inspiration and the center of his life with God and people.[6]

Christ, the gift of the Father's love, is the way to him, the truth into which the Holy Spirit leads us, and the life which he has come to give abundantly.[7]

Secular Franciscans should devote themselves especially to careful reading of the gospel, going from gospel to life and life to the gospel.[8]

5.

Secular Franciscans, therefore, should seek to encounter the living and active person of Christ in their brothers and sisters, in Sacred Scripture, in the Church, and in liturgical activity. The faith of Saint Francis, who often said "I see nothing bodily of the Most High Son of God in this world except his most holy body and blood," should be the inspiration and pattern of their eucharistic life.

Commentary

Chapter Two
Way of Life

4.

The second chapter of the rule is a thorough and detailed description of the Secular Franciscan way of life. The first part (#4-#6) gives the meaning of gospel living in the Franciscan tradition. Then conversion and worship are explained as the necessary preconditions for achieving this gospel life (#7-#8). Finally, paragraphs #9-#19 describe the manner of sharing the Good News of Jesus Christ by how the Secular Franciscans live (#10-#14) and what they do (#15-#19). In the light of scripture and the teachings of Vatican II, this chapter is envisioned as a program for evangelization: how we ourselves are evangelized after the mannr of Francis and secondly how we evangelize others.

Paragraph #4 summarizes the heart of the rule: the very core of gospel life is intimate union with Christ, or in the words of St. Paul, "the life I live now is not my own; Christ is living in me" (Gal 3:20). And so, the Secular Franciscan, alive with the spirit of Francis, knows and experiences the Lord Jesus intensely, binding one's own person with the person of Christ.

5.

As this process develops, then the Secular Franciscan seeks out the living and active person of Christ in all spheres of life: liturgical activity (especially the Eucharist), Scripture, Church, one another (#5). Since the sacrificial union with Christ in the Eucharist is **the** most intense and comprehensive experience of his real presence, this celebration becomes the key encounter, as patterned by Francis himself.

Text

6.

They have been made living members of the Church by being buried and raised with Christ in baptism; they have been united more intimately with the Church by profession. Therefore, they should go forth as witnesses and instruments of her mission among all people, proclaiming Christ by their life and words.

Called like Saint Francis to rebuild the Church and inspired by his example, let them devote themselves energetically to living in full communion with the pope, bishops, and priests, fostering an open and trusting dialogue of apostolic effectiveness and creativity.[9]

7.

United by their vocation as "brothers and sisters of penance,"[10] and motivated by the dynamic power of the gospel, let them conform their thoughts and deeds to those of Christ by means of that radical interior change which the gospel itself calls "conversion." Human frailty makes it necessary that this conversion be carried out daily.[11]

On this road to renewal the sacrament of reconciliation is the privileged sign of the Father's mercy and the source of grace.[12]

Commentary

6.

Sharing Christ's mission through life in the Church is the third point developed on the meaning of gospel living (#6). By word and example the Secular Franciscans bring to those around them the living Christ they have experienced. As it were, they become a living gospel for all to read. This evangelization is based on obedience to the Holy Spirit who inspires and forms the Church, the body of Christ. So, the Secular Franciscans foster an openness to the Spirit and creatively exercise their mission. Furthermore, they hear the call of the Spirit through loyalty, frank dialogue, and cooperation with the legitimate Church authority. This obedience makes ministry authentic and consistent without stifling their creativity.

7.

The next section of the rule (#7 and #8) explains the personal disposition or preconditions (viz., conversion and worship) necessary for achieving the union with Jesus Christ and with one's neighbor described above.

An ongoing change of heart or a continual spiritual renewal is the first condition (#7) for modeling one's own thoughts and deeds on those of Christ. As Francis himself points out in his letter used as the prologue, if we love the Lord with all we are, build a eucharistic community, and remove those things that prevent such union, we become one with him, fulfill the Father's will, and project his image onto the world. Thus, our daily conversion becomes a primary means for putting on Christ and conforming ourselves to him. The sacrament of reconciliation, then, is a privileged means and practical assistance for achieving this objective.

Text

8.

As Jesus was the true worshipper of the Father, so let prayer and contemplation be the soul of all they are and do.[13]

Let them participate in the sacramental life of the Church, above all the Eucharist. Let them join in liturgical prayer in one of the forms proposed by the Church, reliving the mysteries of the life of Christ.

9.

The Virgin Mary, humble servant of the Lord, was open to his every word and call. She was embraced by Francis with indescribable love and declared the protectress and advocate of his family.[14] The Secular Franciscans should express their ardent love for her by imitating her complete self-giving and by praying earnestly and confidently.[15]

10.

United themselves to the redemptive obedience of Jesus, who placed his will into the Father's hands, let them faithfully fulfill the duties proper to their various circumstances of life.[16] Let them also follow the poor and crucified Christ, witness to him even in difficulties and persecutions.[17]

11.

Trusting in the Father, Christ chose for himself and his mother a poor and humble life,[18] even though he valued created things attentively and lovingly. Let the Secular Franciscans seek a proper spirit of detachment from temporal goods by simplifying their own material needs. Let them be mind-

Commentary

8.

The other precondition is to make worship of the Father as central in our own lives as it was in Christ's. The Secular Franciscan, then, communicates and unites with the Lord through the sacraments (again, especially the Eucharist), the liturgy of the hours, contemplation, and any other expression of prayer.

9.

The description of the way of life now moves to the manner of proclaiming the gospel every day by life-style (#10-#14) and ministry or apostolic activity (#15-#19).

First of all, Mary's self-giving and prayer are set up as the primary example of gospel living. Devotion to her has always been a hallmark of the Franciscan calling, both as a way of expressing love for her and as an important way of finding Jesus himself.

10.

The first phase of evangelizing shows how the Secular Franciscans live in this world (#10-#12). Those who go "from gospel to life" have simple living (#10-#12), an experience to togetherness (#13), and selfless service (#14) as qualities of everyday living.

Simple living begins with the choice to unite with Christ so intensely that one is willing to share even his passion: the burdens of hardship and pain within oneself or from outside sources.

11.

Simple living also takes shape (#11) by reducing material needs, by curbing a thirst for possessions and the domineering power that comes from ownership, and by using all God's gifts in a spirit of generosity, justice, and moderation. Gospel poverty for Secular Francis-

Text

ful that according to the gospel they are stewards of the goods received for the benefit of God's children.

Thus, in the spirit of "the Beatitudes," and as pilgrims and strangers on their way to the home of the Father,[19] they should strive to purify their hearts from every tendency and yearning for possession and power.

12.

Witnessing to the good yet to come and obliged to acquire purity of heart because of the vocation they have embraced, they should set themselves free to love God and their brothers and sisters.[20]

13.

As the Father sees in every person the features of his Son, the firstborn of many brothers and sisters,[21] so the Secular Franciscans with a gentle and courteous spirit accept all people as a gift of the Lord[22] and an image of Christ.

A sense of community will make them joyful and ready to place themselves on an equal basis with all people, especially with the lowly for whom they shall strive to create conditions of life worthy of people redeemed by Christ.[23]

14.

Secular Franciscans, together with all people of good will, are called to build a more fraternal and evangelical world so that the kingdom of God may be brought about more effectively. Mindful that anyone "who follows Christ, the perfect man, becomes more of a man himself," let them exercise their responsibilities competently in the Christian spirit of service.[24]

Commentary

cans, then, consists in acquiring possessions justly, keeping needs to a minimum, and using what they have as custodians for the generous benefit of others. In this way they live for the kingdom of God and not for this world according to the charter for happiness given in the "Beatitudes."

12.

The result of simple living in gospel poverty is freedom to seek and share the great treasure of the kingdom: loving God and neighbor (#12).

13.

Hand in hand with simple living is coming to recognize that in Christ all are equally brothers and sisters (#13). There is no room for prejudice or exclusiveness in the Franciscan way of life. In fact, the sense of community and the will toward community compel the Secular Franciscans to discover Christ in everyone, especially the lowly and poor and disadvantaged.

14.

The natural consequence to simple living and a sense of community is selfless service (#14). Secular Franciscans expend themselves by using their special talents, competence and responsibility. Thus they bring to others the experience of God and the hope for achieving their full humanity.

Text

15.

Let them individually and collectively be in the forefront in promoting justice by the testimony of their human lives and their courageous initiatives. Especially in the field of public life, they should make definite choices in harmony with their faith.[25]

16.

Let them esteem work both as a gift and as a sharing in the creation, redemption, and service of the human community.[26]

Commentary

15.

The second grouping (#15-#19) of the ways Secular Franciscans spread the gospel and witness to Jesus Christ deals with concrete action. Not only does gospel living take shape in a special life-style, but also it expresses itself in a specific mode of apostolic activity or ministry.

The first particular aspect of the Secular Franciscans' evangelical action is social justice (#15), both on the individual level and on the level of community participation. They must show justice themselves and motivate justice in others, not just in their private lives, but also in the public forum of politics, business, economics, and the like. This mandate for advancing social justice as an organized group overturns previous prohibitions against a public common expression of rights when it is carried out as a means of demonstrating the convictions of faith.

16.

Another concrete means of proclaiming the Good News of Jesus Christ is expressed in attitudes toward work (#16). Through working the Secular Franciscans discover their workaday world as the arena of their salvation and at the same time exemplify the saving Christ to others. So, human labor is a blessing, both received and bestowed. By working, a person shares in the creative power of the Father, renews the face of the earth along with the Son, and brings the love of the Holy Spirit to the human community. Such an attitude toward work can reshape one's own and others' values and actions regarding labor and management, business and economics, living wage and welfare, proper use of one's own talents and the resources of others.

Text

17.

In their family they should cultivate the Franciscan spirit of peace, fidelity, and respect for life, striving to make of it a sign of a world already renewed in Christ.[27]

By living the grace of matrimony, husbands and wives in particular should bear witness in the world to the love of Christ for his Church. They should joyfully accompany their children on their human and spiritual journey by providing a simple and open Christian education and being attentive to the vocation of each child.[28]

Commentary

17.

A third apostolic expression of gospel living concerns family life (#17). The family is the God-given basic unit of human society and a miniature of the total world already redeemed by Christ. Hence, Franciscan-oriented families present a renewed world of love and dignity, are an example of Christ's love for his Church, and reflect the light of Christ in affront to the darkness of today's shattered families and prevailing godless values. Husbands and wives, then, have a special ministry in the Church to the world. This ministry is exercised in two ways: by leading and educating their children to experience Christ and by witnessing to others that God is present in the family. This Christian family living is one of the most particular expressions of the laity's life and mission in the Church.

Text

18.

Moreover they should respect all creatures, animate and inanimate, which "bear the imprint of the Most High,"[29] and they should strive to move from the temptation of exploiting creation to the Franciscan concept of universal kinship.

Commentary

18.

Ecology (the relationship of creatures with themselves, their environment, and their God) is a fourth expression of the Franciscan apostolate (#18). Francis saw all creation — the sun and moon, the weather and water, fire and earth, forgiving people and death itself — as symbols of the union between God and his people. Hence, all creation has a sacred quality and enjoys a oneness with people in the history of salvation. Following the example of Francis, the Secular Franciscans express a profound respect for all creation and use it for its intended God-given purpose. Furthermore, they ennoble nature and technology and build a community conscience toward using natural resources. This ministry toward creation will stem the selfish tide of abuse and waste and exploitation in this world.

Text

19.

Mindful that they are bearers of peace which must be built up unceasingly, they should seek out ways of unity and fraternal harmony through dialogue, trusting in the presence of the divine seed in everyone and in the transforming power of love and pardon.[30]

Messengers of perfect joy in every circumstance, they should strive to bring joy and hope to others.[31]

Since they are immersed in the resurrection of Christ, which gives true meaning to Sister Death, let them serenely tend toward the ultimate encounter with the Father.[32]

Commentary

19.

A particularly Franciscan ministry is peace-making (#19). Peace grows out of the search for personal integrity and harmony with others and the discovery of God's presence everywhere. It is built up by affirming oneself, seeing others as revealers of God's love, taking a positive approach to solutions, and communicating constantly with the Lord. It is putting aside all thought of violence and embracing a largeness of heart. The result of peace is joy and hope. A special application of this ministry of peace-making is preparation for death at which time a person arrives at that ultimate encounter with God and an eternal peace in his presence that fulfill the earthly quest for peace.

Chapter Three
Life in Fraternity

20.

The Secular Franciscan Order is divided into fraternities of various levels — local, regional, national, and international. Each one has its own moral personality in the Church.[33] These various fraternities are coordinated and united according to the norm of this rule and of the constitutions.

Chapter Three
Life in Fraternity

20.

Ordinarily, the gospel life of Secular Franciscans outlined in the second chapter is developed and sustained within the framework of an organized community, called a fraternity, in each locality. Hence, "fraternity" is the topic of chapter three (#20-#26). These fraternities are living and active communities. They serve as expressions of loving and trusting relationships between members and as a legal unit of government. They exist on various levels and have their own special character (#20). They are given life and direction by their lay leadership and particular characteristics by their local needs (#21). They exist with the approval of the Church (#22) and are nurtured by new members who have been prepared for commitment (#23).

Text | **Commentary**

Their meetings and contributions express their will to and sense of community (#24-#25). Their spiritual growth is developed through the assistance of clergy and religious (#26).

The chapter begins with outlining fraternity as the characteristic of all Secular Franciscan groupings, whether local, regional, provincial, national, or international (#20). A new dimension given to Secular Franciscan life because of this paragraph is an awareness of (and, hence, a mandate to achieve) a fraternity spirit and style operating on levels beyond that of the local fraternity. Regional, provincial, national, or international groupings are not just a federation of independent, semi-autonomous fraternities or a forum for exchange, but actually a fully operating community with its own character, interactivity and authority as defined by the statutes.

21.

On various levels, each fraternity is animated and guided by a council and minister (or president) who are elected by the professed according to the constitutions.[34]

Their service, which lasts for a definite period, is marked by a ready and willing spirit and is a duty of responsibility to each member and to the community.

Within themselves the fraternities are structured in different ways according to the norm of the constitutions, according to the various needs of their members and their regions, and under the guidance of their respective council.

21.

This fraternity is bound together with the leadership of a president and a council who are ready and willing to serve, and it is expressed in diversified ways according to the needs of the area (#21). Two implications ensue from the first part of this paragraph: the importance of choosing available and competent and willing leaders and, secondly, the responsibility of Secular Franciscans themselves to exercise complete control in administrative and temporal matters. The stress on diversified fraternity styles implies that the structure of the community must be tailored to the needs of those who form it.

Text

22.

The local fraternity is to be established canonically. It becomes the basic unit of the whole Order and a visible sign of the Church, the community of love. This should be the privileged place for developing a sense of Church and the Franciscan vocation and for enlivening the apostolic life of its members.[35]

23.

Requests for admission to the Secular Franciscan Order must be presented to the local fraternity, whose council decides upon the acceptance of new brothers and sisters.[36]

Admission into the Order is gradually attained through a time of initiation, a period of formation of at least one year, and profession of the rule.[37] The entire community is engaged in this process of growth by its own manner of living. The age for profession and the distinctive Franciscan sign[38] are regulated by the statutes.

Profession by its nature is a permanent commitment.[39]

Members who find themselves in particular difficulties should discuss their problems with the council in fraternal dialogue.

Withdrawal or permanent dismissal from the Order, if necessary, is an act of the fraternity council according to the norm of the constitutions.[40]

24.

To foster communion among members, the council should organize regular and frequent meetings of the community as well as meeting with other Franciscan groups, especially with youth groups. It should adopt appropriate means for growth in Franciscan and ecclesial life and encourage everyone

Commentary

22.

The local fraternity is the basic living organism of the whole Secular Franciscan Order and a visible sign of the whole Church in miniature (#22). Hence, its beginning and development is guided by Church authority, for it is the center for spiritual growth, apostolic out-reach, and loving union among members. This paragraph calls the members to relate with one another more personally and intensely and stresses the ties with the local bishop.

23.

Paragraph #23 points out the importance of the initial orientation, with elements of both instruction and experience directed toward a life-time commitment in the Order. It also stresses the role of the council in the development of community, especially for new members and for errant members. A number of important implications develop from this paragraph: It is the responsibility of primarily the council (not just the president or the spiritual assistant) to lead new members to commitment and exercise charity in particular difficulties. The life of the whole fraterntiy contributes to the growth of the new members and consolidates it. Furthermore, profession is highlighted as a mature and enduring decision to participate as fully as possible in the Church's lfe and mission according to the manner of Francis.

24.

Paragraph #24 discusses the means to express a strong and lasting fraternity spirit. The regular and frequent meeting (ordinarily once a month) is **the** way to build fraternity with prayer, education, apostolic activity, dialogue and leisure. Continuing education in Franciscanism and Church life is also stressed as a

Text

to a life of fraternity.[41] This communion continues with deceased brothers and sisters through prayer for them.[42]

25.

Regarding expenses necessary for the life of the fraternity and the needs of worship, of the apostolate, and of charity, all the brothers and sisters should offer a contribution according to their means. Local fraternities should contribute toward the expenses of the higher fraternity councils.[43]

26.

As a concrete sign of communion and coresponsibility, the councils on various levels, in keeping with the constitutions, shall ask for suitable and well prepared religious for spiritual assistance. They should make this request to the superiors of the four religious Franciscan families, to whom the Secular Fraternity has been united for centuries.

To promote fidelity to the charism as well as observance of the rule and to receive greater support in the life of the fraternity, the minister or president, with the consent of the council, should take care to ask for a regular pastoral visit by the competent religious superiors[44] as well as for a fraternal visit from those of the higher fraternities, according to the norm of the constitutions.

Commentary

means of spiritual growth and community building. Again, it is emphasized that the fraternity derives much of its life from a vigorous council; hence, the council should meet regularly to take care of ordinary business, foster gospel living, and show concern for the growth of all its members.

25.

Paragraph #25 points out that the voluntary contributions of the members finance the fraternity's spiritual and temporal needs and activities. The fraternity, according to its means and agreed-upon arrangements, also contributes to the support of the regional, provincial, national, and international fraternities. This paragraph is a contemporary application of the traditional Secular Franciscan values outlined in the very first rule that the members are responsible for taking care of their own in whatever way is necessary.

26.

Finally, the rule speaks of the spiritual assistance of the clergy; it also refers to the need of the friars to share fellowship and their Franciscan vocation with the Secular Franciscans (#26). Three important implications are drawn from this paragraph: First of all, since the Secular Franciscan Order is basically a lay order, the laity themselves are primarily responsible for their own spiritual growth and have the duty to get the proper assistance to achieve this end. Secondly, spiritual assistants should have a good background in Franciscanism and Vatican Council II (especially the role of the laity) and a willingness to share their own vocation with the Secular Franciscan community.

The Rule

Text

Thirdly, the official visit to the fraternity is given a dual role: Spiritual growth is ensured through pastoral visitation by a Franciscan friar. Organizational development is provided by the fraternial visitation of a higher lay leader.

"May whoever observes all this be filled in heaven with the blessing of the most high Father, and on earth with that of his beloved Son, together with the Holy Spirit, the Comforter."

(Blessing of St. Francis from the *Testament*)

Notes for the New Rule

1. Known also by the name "The Secular Franciscan Fraternity" or by the abbreviation "T.O.F." which corresponds to Third Order Franciscan.
2. Vatican II, *Lumen Gentium* (Dogmatic Constitution on the Church), 43 (abbr: Church).
3. Pius XII, Allocution to Tertiaries (*"Nel darvi"*), #1 (July 1, 1956): *Acta Apostolicae Sedis* (abbr: AAS), vol. 48, pp. 574-575.
4. Vatican II, *Apostolicam Actuositatem* (Decree on the Apostolate of the Laity), 4m (abbr: Laity).
5. Code of Canon Law, 702:1.
6. 1 Cel 18 (*Omnibus*, p. 244), 115 (*Omnibus*, p. 329) (Abbr: O.).
7. Jn 3:16, 14:6.
8. Laity, 30h.
9. Paul VI, Allocution to Tertiaries (*"Salutiamo volentieri"*), #3 (May 19, 1971): AAS, vol. 63, pp. 545-546.
10. Primitive Rule of the Third Order of St. Francis (abbr: Prim. Rule).
11. Church, 8.
12. Vatican II, *Presbyterorum Ordinis* (Decree on the Ministry and Life of Priests), 18b.
13. Laity, 4a, b, c.
14. 2 Cel 198 (O., p. 521).
15. Church, 67: Laity, 40.
16. Church, 41.
17. Church, 42b.
18. St. Francis, "Letter to All the Faithful," 5 (O., p. 93).
19. Rom 8:17: Church, 48.
20. St. Francis, "Admonitions," 16 (O., p. 83-84); "Letter to All the Faithful," 70 (O., p. 98).
21. Rom 8:29.
22. 2 Cel 85 (O., p. 433); "Letter to All the Faithful," 26 (O., p. 94); 1 OFM Rule, 7:13 (O., p. 38).
23. 1 OFM Rule, 9:3 (O., 39); Mt 25:40.
24. Church, 31; Vatican II, *Gaudium et Spes* (Pastoral Constitution on the Church in the Modern World), 93 (abbr: Church Today).
25. Laity, 14.
26. Church Today, 67:2; 1 OFM Rule, 7:4 (O., p. 37); 2 OFM Rule, 5:1 (O., p. 61).
27. Rule of Leo XIII, 2:8.
28. Church, 41e; Laity, 30b, c.
29. 1 Cel 80 (O., p. 296).
30. Rule of Leo XIII, 2:9; 3 Comp. 14:58 (O., p. 941).
31. St. Francis, "Admonitions," 21 (O., p. 85); 1 OFM Rule, 7:15 (O., p. 38).
32. Church Today, 78:1-2.
33. Code of Canon Law, 687.
34. Code of Canon Law, 687.
35. Pius XII, Allocution to Tertiaries (*"Nel darvi"*), #3 (July 1, 1956); AAS, vol. 48, p. 577.
36. Code of Canon Law, 694.
37. Prim. Rule, 29-30.
38. 1 Cel 22 (O., p. 247).
39. Prim. Rule, 31.
40. Code of Canon Law, 696.
41. Code of Canon Law, 697.
42. Prim. Rule, 23.
43. Prim. Rule, 20.
44. Rule of Nicholas IV, chap. 16.

PART III

CATECHISM

INTRODUCTION

1. What is the official title of the Franciscan Third Order?

The official title of the Franciscan Third Order is now the Secular Franciscan Order, or the Order of Secular Franciscans. The letters S.F.O. are the abbreviation of the title. The Order is also known as the Fraternity of Secular Franciscans, and it may continue to be called Franciscan Third Order.

2. Who approved the present Rule, when and how did it happen?

Pope Paul VI approved the new *Rule of the Secular Franciscan Order* on June 24, 1978, when he promulgated it by the Papal Brief: *The Seraphic Patriarch.*

3. In its history, how many "official" Rules has the Secular Franciscan Order had?

Before this latest Rule, the Secular Franciscan Order has had two different Rules: on August 17, 1289, Pope Nicholas IV promulgated the Rule in the Apostolic Constitution *Supra Montem;* on May 30, 1883, Pope Leo XIII promulgated the second Rule in the Apostolic Constitution *Misericors Dei Filius.*

4. Before these Rules which the Church approved expressly, were there any rules or norms laid down by St. Francis?

The first norms given by St. Francis for the seculars are contained in a short exhortation written by the Seraphic Father entitled *Exhortation of Saint Francis to the Brothers and Sisters in Penance.*

Shortly after the *Exhortation,* St. Francis composed his *Letter to All the Faithful,* in which he further explained and applied what he had written in the *Exhortation.*

In 1221 the Church published a Rule for the "Penance" groups arising in various places. It was known as "Memorial of the Resolutions of the Brothers and Sisters of Penance." It contained 39 articles. It is believed to have been edited by Cardinal Hugolino who later became Pope Gregory IX. St. Francis desired his "Penance group" or secular followers to adopt as their own this "Memorial of Resolutions."

5. Why was it necessary at the present time to formulate a new Rule?

It was thought necessary to formulate a new Rule so that the Secular Franciscan Order would be included in the general renewal of the Church required by the Vatican Council II; and further, to respond to the needs of the modern world.

The original intention of St. Francis has suffered no change nor has it been betrayed by any of the three Rules officially promulgated by the Church. What has been done has been to reform the past, enriching it and adapting it to current needs.

6. How many sections does the New Rule of the Secular Franciscan Order contain?

The New Rule is made up of a PROLOGUE entitled: *Exhortation of St. Francis to the Brothers and Sisters in Penance* and the three chapters: I. - THE SECULAR FRANCISCAN ORDER; II. - THE WAY OF LIFE; III. - LIFE IN FRATERNITY.

PROLOGUE

EXHORTATION OF ST. FRANCIS TO THE BROTHERS AND SISTERS IN PENANCE

1. Where is the Prologue of the new Rule of the Secular Franciscan Order taken from?

From St. Francis himself. This *Exhortation* he wrote to "the Brothers and Sisters in Penance" shortly before his *Letter to All the Faithful.* The authenticity of the *Exhortation* was established by Fr. Cajetan Esser O.F.M. in 1976 after a lengthy and exact critical study. The *Exhortation* is older and shorter than the *Letter.*

2. Why was this *Exhortation* chosen as the Prologue to the Rule?

The *Exhortation* was chosen as the Prologue so that the Secular Franciscans could listen to St. Francis himself and know what the Seraphic Founder had in mind and how he wished his followers to live.

3. What does the *Exhortation* treat of?

It treats about those who do penance and about those who do not want to do penance, explaining in delicate terms and yet with gospel flavor the end-results of the one and the other, calling all to true conversion.

4. Does this *Exhortation* reveal the true spirit of St. Francis?

Indeed it does, for in it St. Francis makes known his own intimate experience of conversion, while showing that his life and Rule are none other than the holy Gospel of our Lord Jesus Christ.

To do penance and to live in accordance with the evangelical norm are the two principal teachings of St. Francis in his *Exhortation to the Brothers and Sisters of Penance.*

CHAPTER ONE

THE SECULAR FRANCISCAN ORDER

1. Who are the Spiritual or Religious Families in the Church?

These are the many different Institutes, Congregations and Religious Orders, which God has given to His Church as an answer to the demands of the times in the course of her history. Such have been the Benedictines, the Mercedarians, Carmelites, Jesuits, Salesians, etc. In this manner God aids His Church in carrying out the work of salvation.

2. Why is it said that these Spiritual or Religious Families in the Church have been raised up by the Holy Spirit?

Because the appearance of each Founder in the history of the Church as well as the history of his Religious Family is believed to be a special charism or divine gift the Church receives from the Holy Spirit. Every Founder carried out the work inspired by the Holy Spirit. The Church examined, tested, and accepted these gifts or charisms. It is in this sense that we understand ecclesiastical approval. In each Founder there is a calling, an inspiration to bring about, along with his followers, a special service to the world and the Church. This calling or inspiration brings them to a distinctive evangelical life. It is precisely this which explains the difference present in the various Institutes or Religious Families in the Church. The Holy Spirit plants in each Religious Family those gifts or charisms necessary to bring about the work committed to it, and encourages it to live the Gospel in a manner that is proper to it (the spirit peculiar to the Institute).

3. Who are those who make up the Franciscan Family?

Fundamentally the Franciscan Family consists of the three Orders: The First Order called the Lesser Brothers or Friars Minor. The Second Order called the Poor Ladies or Poor Clares. The Third Order, originally known as the Brothers and Sisters of Penance and now called the Secular Franciscans.

In the course of time these three Orders spread out into others. The Friars Minor, into the Franciscans, the Conventuals, the Capuchins, and, classified with them, the Third Order Regular, T.O.R. The Poor Clares, into various groups such as the Colettines, Capuchin Poor Clares, Conceptionist Poor Clares.

In modern times numerous Religious Congregations, notably of women, adopted the Rule of the Third Order and constitute the Regular Third Order, as distinct from the Secular Third Order. These congregations consist of Religious men and women who bind themselves by vows, live a common life, and observe the Rule of the Third Order Regular promulgated by Pope Pius XI, on October 4, 1927, in the Apostolic Constitution beginning with the words "Such was the state of affairs." The Franciscan Family, including all branches, is the most numerous Religious Family in the Church. At the present time there are about 36,000 members in the First Order, 22,000 in the Second, 150,000 in the Regular Third Order. The Secular Franciscan Order has about one million and a half members bringing the total Franciscan Family to 1,708,000.

4. What does the statement: "In various ways and forms but in life-giving union with each other," mean?

This means that:

— All the various groups in the Franciscan Family acknowledge St. Francis of Assisi as their common Seraphic Father and Founder.

— In different ways all possess the same charism and Franciscan spirit.

— Any member of the family of God, lay, religious, priest

or member of the hierarchy, can belong to the Franciscan Family, either as a religious or as a lay person (including the secular clergy and members of the hierarchy). Every one of these members also enriches the Franciscan Family, carrying out his particular vocation or particular mission in the Church as the Family of God.

— All accept each other mutually, relate to each other, and complement each other. The Friars and Poor Clares provide their religious experience of the Franciscan way of life for Secular Franciscans, and in turn receive from Lay Franciscans their religious experience of Franciscan living in the world.

Fraternal inter-relations among all members should be encouraged through intense dialogue, organized collaboration, and permanent unifying structures. Foremost among these is the Spiritual Assistance given to the Secular Franciscans by the Friars, the Poor Clares, and the Third Order Regular.

5. How can the Secular Franciscan Order be defined?

The Code of Canon Law (Canon 702) offers the following: "Secular tertiaries are those persons who strive to attain Christian perfection in the world under the guidance and according to the spirit of some Order, in a manner compatible with the secular life, according to the rules approved for them by the Apostolic See."

The new Secular Franciscan Rule contains the following definition, which we will take phrase by phrase and comment on each: "It is an organic union / of all Catholic fraternities scattered throughout the world / and open to every group of the faithful. / In these fraternities the brothers and sisters, led by the Spirit, strive for perfect charity in their own secular state. / By their profession they pledge themselves to live the gospel in the manner of St. Francis by means of this Rule approved by the Church."

6. What is the meaning of: The Secular Franciscan Order is "an organic union"?

It means that the Secular Franciscan Order is an institute within the Church, that it has distinctive characteristic marks, that it contains an internal and complete organization or structure, that it governs itself by norms and laws approved by the Church. The norms or laws that govern the Secular Franciscan Order are: The Code of Canon Law, the Rule of the Secular Franciscan Order, the General Constitutions, and particular Statutes.

7. What is meant by: "The SFO embraces all Catholic fraternities scattered throughout the world?"

The SFO is in every part of the world without limitations of race, nationality, language, or sex.

In Chapter III a careful study will be made of the organization of the SFO which basically is a grouping of the fraternities from regional, provincial, national, and international levels.

To be admitted as a member of the SFO the indispensable condition is to be Catholic. Our Protestant brethren and the Church of England actually have great admiration for St. Francis and some in their own way follow his spirituality. These of course do not belong to the Secular Franciscan Order.

8. What does, "The fraternities of the SFO are open to every group of the faithful" mean?

It means that all Catholics, men, women, children, young and old, single people, married and widowed people are all eligible to be Secular Franciscans.

The General Constitutions establish the conditions for admission to the SFO, such as age, etc.

Members of the hierarchy of the Church (the pope, bishops, priests, and deacons), though not lay persons, may belong to the SFO.

9. What is meant by: "In these fraternities the brothers and sisters, led by the Spirit, strive for perfect charity"?

Those who enter the SFO have a true vocation or charism. Such a vocation or charism is freely granted by the Holy Spirit to whomever He chooses.

It also means that the candidate upon entering the SFO decides to strive after a higher degree of perfection in as far as possible, and thus fulfill the calling of the baptized.

10. What is the meaning of: "The members of the SFO strive after perfect charity in their own secular state"?

Upon entering the SFO, the candidate retains his or her status as a "secular;" but also in that state he or she can and should strive to lead a holy life, for everyone is called to holiness of life. To be a "secular" is not a negative condition which is merely tolerated, but it too is a vocation to be lived and a mission to be accomplished. It is the duty of the "secular" in the Church to handle temporal affairs and order them according to God's designs; it is a vocation proper to him and his particular mission. As a "secular," remaining within the family circle, one must carry out the duties of his or her state of life and take care of the temporal affairs of his or her business and profession.

11. What is to be understood by: "The Secular Franciscans pledge themselves to live the gospel in the manner of St. Francis"?

Through his Profession the candidate makes this pledge before the Church; he or she accepts a real obligation, formal and permanent, to live the gospel after the manner of St. Francis, that is, as Francis understood, lived, and taught it. He or she promises also to observe the Rule and the General Constitutions of the Secular Franciscan Order. The Church, in turn, through the liturgical ceremony of Profession, accepts and blesses, officially and solemnly, the pledge of the Secular Franciscan.

12. Who has the responsibility of giving the official interpretation of the Rule of the Secular Franciscan Order?

The interpretation of the Rule of the Secular Franciscan Order is the exclusive responsibility of the Holy See. When it is necessary, the Holy See gives its interpretations through the Congregation of Religious and Secular Institutes.

Each and every Secular Franciscan should study with eagerness the Rule, understand it correctly, and make it a part of his or her life. Experts in Franciscanism are encouraged to delve deeper into the study of the Rule, making known its history and significance. These findings, however, have only private and scholarly value. They do assist effectively in the knowledge and application of the Rule.

13. Where does one find an authoritative explanation and application of the Rule?

The application of the Rule for the entire Secular Franciscan Order is done through the General Constitutions and in particular Statutes; also in the official commentaries which have been made. The General Constitutions of the SFO, approved on August 25, 1957, are still in force, but they will soon be revised. Particular Statutes are worked out by and for a particular nation, province, or region.

CHAPTER TWO
WAY OF LIFE

1. What does the second chapter of the Rule speak of?

The second chapter of the rule speaks of the spirituality of the Secular Franciscan Order and specifically of the way in which the Secular Franciscan should live. The rule speaks in positive though general terms about the secular Franciscan spirituality.

Continual references are made to the spiritual experience of St. Francis himself and to the way in which we can imitate him in the modern world.

The Rule presents only key ideas and fundamental attitudes. These are to be applied and lived in keeping with th peculiar situation of a given fraternity or an individual Secular Franciscan. We must keep in mind that the Secular Franciscan Order has spread throughout the world and necessarily adapts itself to different mentalities and cultures.

The Rule does not determine small details and thus leaves the doors open to creativity and specifications on the part of the individual brothers and sisters and the fraternities.

2. What is the meaning of: "The rule and life of the Secular Franciscans is this: to observe the gospel of our Lord Jesus Christ"?

It means that the holy gospel of our Lord Jesus Christ

is the foundation and basis of the life of the Secular Franciscan. The gospel is the fountain from which flows all Franciscan spirituality. The holy gospel is "the Good News" of all divine revelation which through salvation history continues to become manifest and attains its culmination in the coming of Christ.

We find this divine revelation or Good News in Sacred Scripture, in the Old as well as in the New Testament. It can be said that the holy gospel comprises the entire Bible. This gospel must be understood in a sense that is ever new and profound and as the Church, inspired by the Holy Spirit, interprets it. The evangelical character of the Secular Franciscan Order gives its members an absolute guarantee, and it also explains its permanence and existence at the present time. It is also the starting point for an in-depth study and correct understanding of its spirituality.

3. What is meant by: "Christ, the gift of the Father's love, is the way to Him, the truth into which the Holy Spirit leads us, and the life which He has come to give abundantly"?

It means that the four Gospels and the entire Bible, with all its teachings, are like a glass through which we can look and a door through which we can enter through. The center is Jesus Christ Himself, His teaching and His life, His entire Person.

The real life of the Secular Franciscan consists in a personal and vital encounter with Jesus Christ, the Lord who satisfies the most profound questions and aspirations of human beings. It also means that the invitation to holiness received by the Secular Franciscan is one to the sharing in the very life of the Most Holy Trinity.

4. How should the Secular Franciscans read the Gospels?

They should read the Scriptures not merely with their bodily eyes and mind, and because of a scholarly interest and curiosity. The Secular Franciscans should approach the Bible with faith, humility, and docility of heart, and listen to the voice of God hidden mysteriously in the sacred pages.

Having attentively listened and understood, they act upon it generously.

In similar fashion the Secular Franciscans seek to find meaning in their daily life, their problems and difficulties, successes and failures, the happenings in the world and history, in the light of the Word of God. That is what "going from gospel to life and life to gospel" implies.

5. Where are the Secular Franciscans to seek the Person of Christ?

Moved by a supernatural spirit, the Secular Franciscans should look for the Person of Christ:

— In *people* who are their brothers and sisters because they are children of the same Father. To them they should generously offer their services and with them work in the building up of a universal fraternity.

— In *Sacred Scripture,* whose principal author is God and contains His Word ever living and present.

— In the *Holy Church,* founded by Jesus Christ and assisted by the Holy Spirit to be the means and sign of salvation of all mankind.

— In *Liturgical Action* where the principal priest or minister is Christ. Liturgical Action re-presents the mysteries of the death and resurrection of Jesus Christ, making us participants.

— The Person of Christ is to be sought above all in *the Eucharist* which, as all the sacraments, imparts grace, and actually contains our Lord Jesus Christ really present in Body, Blood, Soul, and Divinity.

— Finally, Christ must be looked for in creation, in our daily activity, and in natural phenomena.

6. What is the spiritual significance of the Profession of the Secular Franciscan?

The Profession of the Secular Franciscan, though different from Religious Profession, has a deep meaning.

By Profession, the Secular Franciscan renews his or her baptismal vows and his or her consecration to God. He or she attaches himself or herself more fully to the Paschal

Mystery of Christ through the renunciation of sin.

7. What importance does the Church attach to the Profession of the Secular Franciscans?

The Church, on her part, accepts the decision Secular Franciscans make known through Profession, then offers their promise to God in a liturgical prayer and asks that new graces be granted. This action of the Church endorses the decision made by the Secular Franciscans, inserts them more fully into the life of the Church itself, makes them members of the Franciscan Family, and extends to them the riches of its spirituality.

Profession not only influences the interior and personal life of the Secular Franciscans, it also makes of them instruments and witnesses, qualified to teach salvation among men by word and example.

8. What is to be understood by: The Secular Franciscans must live "in full communion with the pope, bishops, and priests fostering an open and trusting dialogue of apostolic effectiveness and creativity"?

Secular Franciscans must offer obedience, loyalty, and loving service to the hierarchy, that is, to those vested with ecclesiastical authortiy: the pope, the bishops and the priests.

They must accept, without reservation, the Catholic doctrines and the sacraments of the Church, and show reverence towards sacred things and places.

They should be at the disposal of the hierarchy and sincerely willing to take part in pastoral and community action in the diocese and the parish to which they belong.

They accept the Secular Franciscan Order in the form chosen and approved by the Church, joyfully submit to its laws, and promote its renewal.

9. What does conversion or radical interior change mean?

In the first place, it must be said that conversion or "penance" cannot be restricted to external acts of mortification. Nor can we reduce it to a mere change of interior attitude or outlook, such as a new way of thinking. It implies something much more broad and profound. A true conversion is a complete change in a person, so deep and intimate that it can transform his or her external behavior as well. Conversion means the complete surrender of our whole being to God who has an absolute claim over us.

The Sacrament of Reconciliation, or confession, is the means instituted by Jesus Christ to make possible and bring about such a conversion in every Christian. Consequently, Secular Franciscans should frequently go to confession.

10. What is the meaning of: The Secular Franciscans should "let prayer and contemplation be the soul of all they are and do"?

The Secular Franciscans, true Christians that they are, should make of their entire life or the whole of their activity one continuous prayer. Secular Franciscans must practice all the kinds of prayer the Church uses; vocal prayer and mental prayer, the prayer of petition, the prayer of thanksgiving, the prayer of expiation, and the prayer of praise. They should also pray humbly to God for the grace of contemplation.

Secular Franciscans must above all take active part in the liturgical prayer of the Church because of its dignity and value. They should, whenever possible, take part in the daily celebration of Holy Mass and the fruitful reception of Holy Communion.

Although the recitation of the Twelve Our Fathers is no longer prescribed as the Office, it may continue to serve as such. The Liturgy of the Hours, which is the official and public prayer of the Church, offered daily in the name of Christ Himself to the heavenly Father, is expressly recommended to Secular Franciscans, "in one of the forms proposed by the Church," which include approved shorter and partial forms of the Office.

11. How should the Secular Franciscans manifest their ardent love and devotion to the Virgin Mary?

Devotion to the Blessed Virgin Mary by the Secular Franciscans is evident most of all in the imitation of her virtues. In keeping with the gospel, the preeminent virtue of the Virgin Mary is her unconditional surrender of self in accepting and carrying out the word of God. Mary was a most docile instrument carrying out God's plan in her regard.

The Secular Franciscans further show love and devotion to the Blessed Virgin through prayer, particularly the Angelus, the recitation of the Rosary or the Franciscan Crown (Rosary of the Seven Joys), and other Marian devotions distinctive of the Franciscan family.

12. What does the Rule teach concerning obedience?

Principally, the rule says that the Secular Franciscans unite themselves to Christ by total obedience to the will of the Father. Christ's obedience went so far as to submit to His redemptive passion and death.

Total obedience means compliance with God's will, not only in those matters pertaining to His commandments, but also those which He desires or advises.

Secular Franciscans must fulfill the duties of his state of life, the requirements and directives of legitimate superiors either in the Order, in the Church, in civic affairs, in the home, and at work. He accepts joyfully all that occurs in his daily life, because whatever happens either comes from God or is permitted by God for our benefit.

Obedience should always be inspired by a supernatural motive. One obeys to please God and not man.

13. What does the Rule teach concerning poverty?

It teaches primarily that Secular Franciscans should maintain a balanced relation to material goods, not allowing the heart to become attached to them and using them as God requires and wishes. Private ownership and wealth are not ends in themselves, rather they are means to provide food, clothing, and shelter. They are means to serve God and our neighbor and in that way to attain our final goal and eternal reward.

Poverty consequently requires that we regard and use material goods, not as the absolute possession of the individual who has them, but rather as goods entrusted to us by God for management. God will require an accounting of the manner in which we use and administer them.

14. What does the Rule teach concerning purity?

Since the Secular Franciscan can be either a married person, single, or widowed, the Rule uses the terms "purity of heart" with reference to chastity.

Chastity or purity is the intelligently restrained use of the gift of sex according to God's law. This concept is applicable to the purity expected in all states of life. Chastity or purity in the matrimonial vocation will differ from that of unmarried members. The main emphasis of the rule lies in the motives and purposes of chastity: to proclaim to the world that greater and more important blessings lie in the future and to free man from mere carnal love that he may the better serve God and his fellow man.

15. What does the Rule teach concerning fraternity?

Thus far the explanations given pertained to what has been called "the evangelical values" of the Rule. Now begins the exposition of "the human values" of the Rule. This distinction actually is merely a conceptual one. In practice these values are equally important, they complement each other and should be acted upon simultaneously as St. Francis did when loving Christ his Lord and Master and at the same time caring for his brothers the lepers.

Chapter Three of the Rule, which is titled: "Life in Fraternity," speaks of the organization or structure of each fraternity or group of members; but Chapter Two speaks of fraternity as an attitude or disposition toward all men. Fraternity, of its nature, tends to be universal and to reach beyond family limits. Since all men are our brothers, fraternity embraces all humanity. True fraternity has for its goal the love of every human being without distinction, regardless of social standing or political ideas or religious beliefs.

The Secular Franciscan exemplifies this fraternity in hundreds of ways: living in the midst of people, he shows himself ready to be of service and help all in need. He accepts all men in a positive and optimistic attitude. He cultivates and practices the human virtues, such as simplicity, courtesy, graciousness, and chivalry.

16. What does the statement that the Secular Franciscans "are called to build a more fraternal and evangelical world" mean?

The Rule expects the Secular Franciscans to feel completely that they are citizens of the world, inserted in its very history and solicitously concerned with its complex social phenomena, its politics, its cultures, etc.

In proper perspective, the Secular Franciscan must keep abreast of the current progress (social, scientific, and technical) of humanity. This progress in line with spiritual values promotes the achievement of the Kingdom of God in the present world and gives some indication of the world to come.

The Secular Franciscan must be conscious of the grave problems that beset the present generations such as hunger, unemployment, social injustices, etc.

These problems must be investigated and studied under the light of the principles that arise from the truth about God, Christ, man and the world.

The study and reflection concerning these matters can be realized through a systematic and organized study of the doctrines of the Church regarding them. It can also happen through the observation of every day life around us with all the accompanying consequences. These studies and reflections should result in practical and concrete conclusions.

17. How can the Secular Franciscans become involved in the promotion of social justice?

The Secular Franciscan must always make a clear choice favoring the rights of every human being. He must promote the dignity of the "whole man" and all mankind while demanding complete freedom from segregation and subjugation. Problems in matters of social justice are often very serious in our present times and demand conscientious, forceful, and effective initiatives by individuals and groups enlightened by faith and guided by the teaching authority of the Church.

Because it is not easy to determine the mood or conduct of individuals in given situations or circumstances, the Secular Franciscan, after evaluating the situation as accurately as possible, must have recourse to the teachings of the Church in that specific field, and then faithfully and with enthusiasm apply her directives.

"The testimony of their human lives" mentioned in the Rule is the best contribution a Secular Franciscan can make in matters of justice, and this does not allow exemptions.

This testimony of life is equal to the evangelical preaching about love. Social problems are solved only by and with the fire of Christian love.

18. What should the attitude of the Secular Franciscan be toward work?

He should look upon work not as a penalty nor unbearable burden but as a blessing bestowed by God in order to develop human creativity. In fact, human labor no matter how humble and plain or noble and astounding, should be looked upon as the continuation of the work of the Creator, as a favor to the worker's brothers, and finally as a personal carrying out and fulfillment of God's plan in history.

God created man that he might develop and produce results. With his labor, as a secondary cause, man develops what God has created, giving it significance and new values. In a certain sense, by working, man re-creates the things he makes. Moreover, when performed in the state of grace and expressly offered to God, work assumes great value.

19. What is the message of the Rule concerning marriage and family life?

An entire article is devoted to marriage and family life precisely because a great number of Secular Franciscans belong to that state of life.

Franciscan husbands and wives are to seek holiness through a harmony of mind and heart, mutually encouraging each other in trials and good times to a faithful imitation of Christ.

The fulfillment of the duties of their state of life makes up their work of sanctification. Such are good example, for and with their children, in their daily work and prayer, in an atmosphere of mutual dependence and understanding; also, the attention given to a responsible human and Christian formation of their offspring as well as the direction of their children toward a vocation in life; and, finally, the sharing of their spiritual blessings with other families, even to the point of apostolic action.

20. How should the Secular Franciscan feel towards all creatures animate and inanimate?

Francis of Assisi, the saint of universal brotherhood, who called all creatures "brothers and sisters," must be the model for the Secular Franciscan.

Inspired by faith, the Secular Franciscan looks upon all creation as God's first manifestation of Himself to man and the clear and brilliant reflection of divine glory. It is precisely in this way that he seeks to encounter Christ, through and for whom all creation exists.

Every effort should be made by the Secular Franciscan to stop irresponsible encroachment on nature, notably in the expansion of cities and in industrialization. For, we are not only to benefit by nature but we must also protect and preserve and develop it.

According to the Franciscan concept, creatures are the "imprint of the divine footsteps."

21. Regarding peace, what does the Rule ask of the Secular Franciscan?

They should be promoters of peace in the Fraternity, in the home, in the society surrounding them, and even among nations. This they do through word of mouth, through deeds and external behavior. Peace is the product of justice, and the means of attaining it are respect for all mankind and the practice of fraternal love.

The Secular Franciscan is motivated by the evangelical attitude of meekness, helpfulness, and dialogue rather than confrontation and a spirit of overlording it over others. Such dialogue, initiated by the Secular Franciscan, shows no pretense of a "know-it-all" approach in matters beyond his or her competency, instead of inquiries and explanations that can clarify the problems discussed. Among Secular Franciscans there may be some with expertise in certain situations who may and should offer assistance for practical solutions.

In the event that differences arise among the brethren, the Secular Franciscan should be the first to make the move to bring about peace and harmony.

Secular Franciscans who have been blessed with material goods should, in good time, make a will and thus preclude any occasion of ill-will and discord among members of the family.

22. How should the Secular Franciscan promote holy joy?

Christian joy presupposes and surpasses natural joy. Christian joy results from interior peace of conscience, and is the fruit of good works. It comes from a sense of being safely in God's hands, and from the firm hope for eternal life.

Perfect joy is found in bearing trials for Christ, above all in sickness and adversity; and in a simple and holy life.

Though true joy does not necessarily consist of smiles and laughter, the Secular Franciscan ought to manifest his joy and prudently show graciousness toward all.

He should help his neighbor face and overcome life's problems and difficulties while showing him how to enjoy daily blessings.

He should speak to sinners of the joy of returning to God.

Franciscan joy should be kind to the sick and the elderly, not merely as a token of sympathy, but as an aid in evaluating and alleviating their suffering. Those suffering while in the state of grace are continuing and fulfilling Christ's Passion.

23. What does the Rule teach concerning death?

The conclusion of Chapter Two refers to death. Death is a reality which no one can escape. A Christian is incorporated into Christ through baptism; in death, the Christian is fully immersed into Christ's death and resurrection.

Even as St. Francis, the Secular Franciscan must welcome "Sister Death" with Christian serenity and true joy, knowing it is not the end but rather a transformation from earthly and passing existence into eternal and real life.

CHAPTER THREE
LIFE IN FRATERNITY

1. What does chapter three of the Rule treat of?

Chapter Three of the Rule deals with the internal organization of the entire Secular Franciscan Order and of the individual Fraternities that make up the Order.

To appreciate this chapter properly the following observations should be kept in mind:

(a) The general directives proposed by the Rule are to be amplified and ultimately to be adapted concretely in the General Constitutions and particular Statutes. This explains the apparent inconclusiveness of a few of the articles of the Rule.

(b) In our present discussion of the general principles of the third chapter of the Rule we shall not refer to the old: "Constitutions of the Third Order Secular of St. Francis," promulgated in 1957. As was mentioned in Chapter One, these Constitutions are in process of revision and will soon be updated.

(c) For the present, the "directives" of the new Rule will be explained from the point of view of the documents of the Church and the Order explicitly cited in the present Rule.

2. What is the basic group of the Secular Franciscan Order?

The various Fraternities make up the Secular Franciscan Order. Individually, each Fraternity is a cell of the Church and the Order.

Each one of the Fraternities is a moral person within

the Church enjoying privileges and bound by obligations in conformity with the Code of Canon Law.

Fraternities are organized and grouped according to provincial, regional, national, and world-wide levels.

3. Who constitute the governing body of a Fraternity?

The governing body of a Fraternity (local, regional, provincial, international) consists of a Minister (known also as the President) and a Council.

The office of Minister (President) occupies the first place. This Minister/President is elected by the professed members of the Fraternity in question, as prescribed by the General Constitutions.

Although no specific period of duration is set for this office it is spoken of as being temporary.

Upon acceptance of the office, the Minister/President is given the commitment and responsibility of "ministering" and to the best of his/her ability governing all the members and the entire Fraternity. The title "Minister" implies just that, namely "servant."

The Minister/President is assisted by a Council in the government of the Fraternity.

4. How is a local Fraternity established?

For the existence of a local Fraternity there must be a canonical erection, namely, all the requirements mentioned in the Code of Canon Law must be carried out faithfully, step by step. These are: approval by the local bishop, given in writing; a document of erection, bearing the signature of the authorized superior of the First Order or his representative (spiritual assistant), etc.

5. What is the meaning of "local Fraternity"?

A local Fraternity, even when small in membership, is a cell in the entire Order because it is recognized and approved by the Church, has legitimate officers, and seeks to live the Franciscan way of life. It can, therefore, be said that it truly is a part of the Order.

In the same manner, a local Fraternity is a cell of the

entire Church. It is truly a part of the Church.

In a local Fraternity it is possible to live and share the life of the Church and the Franciscan vocation. It can be the spring-board for many tremendous apostolic activities.

6. Who admits members into the Secular Franciscan Order?

Petitions of admission must be presented to the local Fraternity, and the Council of that Fraternity decides whether or not to accept the candidate.

The official admission of a candidate is recorded in the Register of the Fraternity.

7. What is the procedure of becoming a member of a Fraternity?

After the Council admits a candidate there are three phases to be observed in the process of becoming a Secular Franciscan. They are: Initiation (Postulancy); Formation (Novitiate); and, finally, Profession of the Rule. The new Rule contains nothing with regard to Initiation. It leaves it up to the General Constitutions to set down directives.

8. Are there any rules set down for the period of formation?

The only statement of the Rule is that the period of Formation should last for at least one year.

9. Who is responsible for the guidance and formation of the candidates?

The entire Fraternity is committed to and responsible for the development and spiritual growth of the candidates. The whole Fraternity is bound to form its candidates through studies and exemplary lives. Over and above this it is the specific duty of the Master of Novices and the Assistant Master designated by the Council of the Fraternity.

10. What is the required age for professing the Rule of the Secular Franciscan Order?

The Rule does not specify a definite age. This is left to the particular Statutes.

11. Does the Rule say anything concerning the "habit" or some other symbol or distinctive Franciscan sign?

In this matter also, the Rule says nothing definitely, but leaves it up to the particular Statutes.

12. For what period of time is the Profession made?

Of its very nature, profession is a permanent commitment — for life.

13. How are difficulties that arise within the Fraternities to be resolved?

Problems that arise among the members of a Fraternity may be brought to the attention of the Council, by whom they may be discussed in fraternal dialogue unless discretion and prudence suggest otherwise.

14. Is it permitted to expel a professed member from the Fraternity?

Only in very serious cases and that after all other means — legal and evangelical — such as counseling, admonition, and penances, have been to no avail.

The process of dismissal and definitive expulsion is within the competence of the Council of the Fraternity exclusively, and must be carried out in strict compliance with the norms of the General Constitutions.

15. How should fraternal life be encouraged among the members?

The Rule places great importance on the good works that bring the members together and asks that these be cultivated in every way possible.

Regular and frequent meetings are mentioned in the Rule.

The regular meetings spoken of refer to the customary gatherings of the members of a Fraternity. These may be held once a week, as is the custom in some localities, or once a month on a definite Sunday. Gatherings of the members of a Fraternity may be arranged also for special festivals or anniversaries. The term "frequent meetings" has reference also to conventions attended by members of various Fraternities; for instance, members of the Fraternities of a city, a region, a diocese, a province, or a nation.

Conventions may be organized in conjunction with other Franciscan families, such as the friars of the First Order, nuns of the Second Order, and religious of the Third Order Regular.

Reunions or conventions are organized for the spiritual and educational benefit of the members through common prayer and conferences and dialogue. The Rule insists that they be organized primarily for the promotion and increase of fraternal life.

With the same idea in mind the Rule mentions the deceased members. These members continue to be our brethren, for whom we have a grave duty to offer our prayers and spiritual suffrages.

16. How does the Rule provide for the defrayment of necessary expenses of local fraternities and organizations of fraternities?

The Rule states that contributions to the Fraternity should be made according to the means of each member. Those enjoying greater material blessings should contribute more and those with less may give less.

17. How is the Fraternity to use the contributions of its members?

These offerings should be used in the first place to defray the internal expenses of the Fraternity: namely, office upkeep, travel of directors, library materials, correspondence, etc. In the second place, for the religious activities of the Fraternity, for example, stipends for Masses for deceased members. Also, apostolic and charitable enterprises, the missions, catechetical materials, medicine and clinical needs of the poor, etc.

18. Do the Fraternities have an obligation to contribute to the support of higher councils?

Local Fraternities have the duty to contribute to higher

councils (Provincial, National, International) to assist in meeting the many expenses they incur in behalf of the Secular Franciscan Order. Because these councils bear a responsibility for the spiritual welfare of the Order and promote its apostolic endeavors, justice requires they receive material assistance so that they can carry out their tasks.

The General Constitutions and the particular Statutes will determine the ways and means of gathering and delivering such funds.

19. From whom does the Secular Franciscan Order receive spiritual assistance?

Because of the unity of the Franciscan Family and to manifest more concretely the communion and co-responsibility of the entire family of St. Francis, the spiritual assistance of the Secular Franciscan Order comes from the superiors of the four Franciscan Families known as the Franciscans, the Conventuals, the Capuchins, and the Third Order Regular (T.O.R.).

20. What is the role of the friars of the First Order and Third Order Regular appointed as the Spiritual Assistants to the Secular Franciscan Order?

These friars assist the Fraternities of the Secular Franciscans, not as directors nor as superiors, but rather as brothers and fellow pilgrims called to the same charismatic life of St. Francis. For this reason these are no longer called spiritual directors, but spiritual assistants.

The Spiritual Assistant to the Secular Franciscans ought to be:

A sign and witness to the Franciscan charism through his understanding and knowledge of Franciscan spirituality and the examplary living of it. He is vigilant in insuring the loyal and continual observance of the charism of St. Francis by the Secular Franciscans.

He is an "older brother" of Secular Franciscans, providing spiritual assistance and advice in their Franciscan life by encouraging and inspiring them in their apostolate. If he is a priest, the assistant also has the duty of instructing his brothers in the Faith. The administration of the Fraternity remains the responsibility of the Fraternity itself.

Finally, the Spiritual Assistant should be a channel or bond of union and a channel of communication between the First Order and Third Order Regular on the one hand and the Secular Franciscan Order on the other.

21. What is the procedure in requesting a Spiritual Assistant?

Any friar of the First Order or Third Order Regular, be he a priest or a brother, may be assigned as a Spiritual Assistant. Obviously, he should have a suitable knowledge and love of the Secular Franciscan Order.

It is up to the Councils, local, provincial, national, and international, to request of the superiors of the First Order and Third Order Regular to provide qualified assistants to help and guide them.

22. How many kinds of visitations of the Fraternities does the rule speak of?

The Rule no longer speaks of "canonical visitations." Instead, it mentions two types of visitations: "pastoral" and "fraternal."

The "pastoral visitation" is that of the First Order or Third Order Regular to the Fraternities. This visitation is requested of the proper superior by the Minister (President) with the approval of the Council. The Rule does not fix a definite time for requesting a pastoral visitation of a Fraternity.

The purpose of the pastoral visitation is: first to evaluate the fidelity of the Secular Franciscans in observing the Franciscan charism; and, then, to examine their observance of the Rule, and to encourage the spiritual and apostolic development of the Fraternity.

The "fraternal visitation" is that of a higher Council of the Secular Franciscans to a Fraternity. The request for such a visitation is presented to the higher Council itself, in keeping with the directives of the General Constitutions.

PART IV

INSTRUCTIONS

PREFACE

St. Francis of Assisi became the instrument of the Holy Spirit in bringing about a renewal within the Church of the thirteenth century. Countless thousands, from pope to simple peasant, responded to his graphic and intense imitation of the earthly life of Jesus Christ. He has given us an example of what gospel-living truly means.

Pope Pius XI in his Encyclical *Rite Expiatis* (1926) acknowledged that St. Francis of Assisi was the most perfect imitator of Jesus Christ that has ever lived. He was truly a mirror of Christ.

Francis has left the Church a legacy in the three Orders which he founded: the Friars Minor (men religious), the Poor Clares (cloistered women religious), and his penitents (laity of both sexes, married and single, and secular clergy). In the course of the centuries other religious groups have adopted St. Francis as their father. All these form the Franciscan family and are responsible to keep his influence alive in the Church.

The largest part of this family is the secular form of Franciscan life, namely, the Secular Franciscan Order. It is especially for those considering a vocation to the Secular Order that the two series of instructions presented here are intended. However, they will prove of benefit to all who wish to understand the spirit of the Little Poor Man of Assisi.

Fr. Zachary Grant O.F.M.Cap.
General Editor

INTRODUCTION

To those who feel called by God to serve Christ and his Church in the footsteps of St. Francis of Assisi as Secular Franciscans.

To enter the Order you must apply to the Minister (or President) of a Secular Franciscan fraternity (community). When accepted as a candidate, you will undergo a time of initiation. This will last about six months, often longer. If satisfied that you show positive signs of a Franciscan vocation and that your attitude indicates a proper understanding of the Order's purpose, the council of the fraternity will admit you to a period of formation.

During this period you will be trained in Christian virtue and instructed in the Secular Franciscan Rule and the Franciscan way of life. The period of formation must last at least one year before the council can admit you to Profession of the Rule. This means a permanent commitment as a member of the Order.

These instructions which follow are divided into two series: six lessons for the time of initation (series one) and twelve lessons for the period of formation (series two). That averages out to a minimum of one lesson per month.

Each instruction contains a *basic* lesson on the spirit of the Order and the Christian way of life for Secular Franciscans. What we offer is the "raw material" for each lesson, namely, quotations from Scripture, the documents of the II Vatican Council, and the original Franciscan sources. Also included in each instruction are appropriate excerpts from the Secular Franciscan Rule, and a lesson orientation which gives the Franciscan focus.

The material included here shall be considered only the most fundamental instruction needed by all. Obviously, each candidate should receive as much instruction as can be absorbed. Hence, the instructor will use additional material, or require supplementary reading. For this purpose a bibliography is provided.

It may seem elementary, but we would like to emphasize that the course of study in the Franciscan Rule must be integrated into a complete program of formation and sustained by prayer.

REFERENCES

The Scripture passages are taken from *The New American Bible* translation. Where additional references are given, the abbreviations used are:

Old Testament: Gn - Genesis

New Testament: Mt - Gospel of Saint Matthew
Mk - Gospel of Saint Mark
Lk - Gospel of Saint Luke
Jn - Gospel of Saint John
Ac - Acts of the Apostles
Rm - Epistle to the Romans
ICr - First Epistle to the Corinthians
IICr - Second Epistle to the Corinthians
Gl - Epistle to the Galatians
Ph - Epistle to the Ephesians
Cl - Epistle to the Collosians
IPt - First Epistle of Saint Peter
IJn - First Epistle of Saint John
Rv - Revelations

References to the Second Vatican Council documents are quoted from *Vatican Council II* by Austin Flannery O.P., and abbreviated thus:

Ap - Decree on the Apostolate of the Laity
Bs - Decree on Bishops
Ch - Constitution on the Church
Lt - Constitution on the Sacred Liturgy
MW - Constitution on the Church in the Modern World
Pr - Decree on the Ministry and Life of Priests
Rl - Decree on the Renewal of Religious Life

Rule of the Secular Franciscan Order

The original Franciscan writings are quoted from *St. Francis of Assisi: Omnibus of Sources,* edited by Marion A. Habig O.F.M., published by Franciscan Herald Press, Chicago, Illinois 60609, 1972. Abbreviations used are:

Ad - Admonitions of Saint Francis
IC - First Life of Celano
IIC - Second Life of Celano
CS - Canticle of Brother Sun (St. Francis)
Fa - Letter to All the Faithful (St. Francis)
Fl - Little Flowers of Saint Francis
Mj - Major Life of Saint Francis by Saint Bonaventure
MP - Mirror of Perfection
OF - Paraphrase of the Our Father (St. Francis)
Pr - Legend of Perugia
PV - Praise of the Virtues (St. Francis)
SC - Sacrum Commercium: Francis and His Lady Poverty
3C - Legend of the Three Companions
TO - First Rule of the Third Order
VM - Salutation of the Blessed Virgin

BIBLIOGRAPHY

Biographical:

St. Francis of Assisi: Omnibus of Sources, by Marion A. Habig O.F.M.

Lives of St. Francis by Thomas of Celano
Lives of St. Francis by St. Bonaventure
Legend of the Three Companions
Legend of Perugia
Mirror of Perfection
Little Flowers of St. Francis

The Poverello, by Mark Hegener O.F.M.
St. Francis of Assisi, by Omer Englebert
St. Francis of Assisi, by Johannes Jorgensen
Mirror of Christ, by Isidore O'Brien O.F.M.
St. Francis of Assisi (interpretive), by G. K. Chesterton
Francis: The Journey and the Dream (interpretive), by Murray Bodo O.F.M.

Bibliography

Instructional:

Call to Commitment in the School of St. Francis by Aeby, Delesty, and Chaignat O.F.M.Cap.

The Third Order Vocation, by Leonard Foley O.F.M., and Jovian Weigel O.F.M.

Formation of Lay Franciscans, by Philip Marquard O.F.M.

Short History of the Third Order, by Marion A. Habig O.F.M. and Mark Hegener O.F.M.

The Franciscan Herald (monthly magazine) from the Franciscan Herald Press

Formative:

Spirit and Life, by Heribert Roggen O.F.M.

The Franciscan Charism in the Church, by Anselm W. Romb O.F.M.Conv.

Living Our Future: Francis of Assisi and the Church Tomorrow by Mario Von Galli S.J.

The Third Order For Our Times, by Auspicius Van Corstanje O.F.M.

Take Time For Sunsets, by Lester Bach O.F.M.Cap.

Watering the Seed by Luke Ciampi O.F.M.

Francis: Bible of the Poor, by Auspicius Van Corstanje O.F.M.

The First Franciscans and the Gospel, by Duane V. Lapsanski

A Poor Man's Peace, by Ephrem Longpre O.F.M.

Meditations on the Gospels, from Precious Blood Monastery, Brooklyn

Meditations on the Epistles of St. Paul, from Precious Blood Monastery, Brooklyn

I
INSTRUCTIONS FOR POSTULANTS
From Rome to Assisi

Our Journey begins at Rome. Fortified with the approval of the Apostolic See, and confident that we are thus united with Christ, we set forth toward Assisi. There we will learn from Francis his way of fulfilling the command of our Lord "to proclaim the kingdom of God and penance."

These chapters, studied during the time of initiation (which is often called postulancy), give the basic knowledge for a mature request to become a Secular Franciscan. The candidate (postulant) must have more than a vague idea of what a Secular Franciscan vocation means. These are the basic requirements:

(a) knowledge of St. Francis himself;
(b) an understanding of the Order's purpose;
(c) a desire to be part of a community;
(d) a strong feeling for the Franciscan spirit, as revealed in the Secular Franciscan Rule;
(e) a sense of "being called by God" to this way of life.

We begin with St. Francis since he is our model. The man himself must be understood; otherwise one cannot comprehend the Franciscan spirit or Franciscan spirituality. Therefore, it is important that the candidate read a more extensive biography than is presented here. And, since the Franciscan life is a radical living of the gospel, the candidate should also use the four gospels as daily meditation, particularly that of St. Matthew.

1

WHO IS THIS FRANCIS OF ASSISI?

The Early Life of Saint Francis

In no other Order does its spirit flow from the founder himself more than in the Franciscan Order. Unless we experience the warmth and enthusiasm of Francis' love for Jesus Christ, there will be no practical effect on our Christian life. First we must look to his origins as a man of his times and to the circumstances that formed his unique personality.

His Youth

St. Francis was born at Assisi in Umbria in 1181 or the beginning of 1182, the son of Peter Bernardone, a rich cloth merchant, and his wife, Donna Pica, possibly a Provencal noble woman.

Peter, absorbed in business, left the early education of the child to his wife, a woman of great virtue. She devoted herself to her son's spiritual training, and thus sowed the seeds for his future holiness. With a rudimentary knowledge of Latin, he learned to read, write, and count, solely in virtue of the commercial career his father had in mind for him. At about the age of fifteen he entered his father's business, and quickly displayed the traits of a shrewd, practical merchant.

At the same time the chivalry of the age fascinated him. He yearned for the accolade of knighthood. Falling into worldly ways, he followed the zests of his temperament, so eager for renown and pleasure. Francis quickly became the idol of Assisi's youth, both for the delightfulness of his company and the profligacy with which he lavished his doting father's money on boon companions. These were the sinful years for which he would do severe penance for the rest of his life.

His Conversion

A year's incarceration as a military prisoner, and a long, debilitating illness, seem to have prepared the way for his conversion. Then God began to intervene in extraordinary ways. Still hoping to be dubbed knight on a battle field, Francis had joined the expedition of Walter of Brienne into Apulia. The Lord's voice spoke to him one night out of the darkness, telling him to return to his native town, there to receive further enlightenment concerning his future.

Francis immediately returned to Assisi. His heart was no longer on fine clothes, gold or silver, or revelry with his friends. The loving attraction he must have felt for the Savior since childhood now flared up into an overwhelming personal love for Jesus. His chosen friends now were the poor and the outcasts. He envied them. He exchanged clothes with one of them in order to experience extreme poverty at first hand. He even disgraced himself by begging scraps of food from his neighbors' doors. He embraced and cared for lepers, who formerly were abhorrent to him. He wanted nothing so much as to imitate Christ as he found Him poor and suffering in the Gospel.

Derided by his former friends, and stoned by street urchins as a madman, he brought upon himself the terrible wrath of his father. Peter Bernardone cruelly beat and cursed his son who had brought such dishonor to his house. Meanwhile, Francis fasted and prayed and endured the mystical dark nights. Still, he could not discover what the Lord specifically desired of him.

A Hermit's Life

One day while praying in the dilapidated chapel of San Damiano on the outskirts of Assisi, Christ spoke to him from the crucifix: "Francis, go, repair my house, which, as you can see, is falling completely to ruin." Not understanding that these words referred to his mission of rebuilding the Church through the great return to gospel values he was to set in motion, he took the command literally. He immediately sold goods and a horse, which were his father's property, to finance the restoration of San Damiano. He himself collected stones and set to work as a laborer.

Brought by his father before the bishop of Assisi, Francis took the opportunity to renounce his family inheritance and all earthly goods, turning for protection and care to his Father in heaven. Francis had committed himself totally to the service of God. The bishop made him ward of the Church and ever afterward cherished and assisted him. This happened in the year 1206.

For two years Francis led a hermit's life, garbed as a pilgrim, repairing churches in and about Assisi, including the chapel of Our Lady of the Angels, also known as Portiuncula, the "Little Portion," in the valley below the town. It was here that he came to the full realization of his personal vocation in the year 1208. It occurred as he heard the Gospel read at Mass in which Our Lord enjoins upon the Apostles extreme poverty in dress, forbids them to receive silver, gold, or money, and sends them through the world to preach the Kingdom of God and penance. Francis laid aside his pilgrim's garb and shoes, fashioned for himself a course habit in the shape of a cross, girded it with a rope, and began to preach.

The Brotherhood Forms

It was not long before disciples flocked to him, the first being Bernard of Quintavalle, a rich young Assisian, who gave all his wealth to the poor. As a guide to their observance of the Gospel Francis composed a short rule of life for his new brothers, and in the year 1209 he journeyed to Rome with the first eleven of them to have their way of life approved by the Pope. Innocent III received them kindly. After some hesitation — for a number of cardinals thought their program highly impractical and dangerous — His Holiness confirmed their Rule orally, with a promise of final ratification in the future as the number of friars grew. He also granted them permission to preach penance to the faithful. Francis and his brothers then pronounced the vows of religion. Thus the little company became a religious order, the First Order of St. Francis, to be known as the Friars Minor.

Back in Assisi Francis and his companions preached with wonderful success. Soon they were on preaching tours throughout Italy making peace, inducing sinners to repent and return to the sacraments, and influencing all to observe the moral teachings of the Savior, especially the practice of charity and forgiveness.

Their preaching was marked by the loyalty they instilled in the people to the teachings of the Church, and to her pastors, especially the Vicar of Christ. Francis became known as the "man wholly Catholic and totally apostolic" (*apostolic* referring to his extraordinary devotion to the Apostolic Lord, the Pope). Whereas he went as far as to be ordained deacon, he did not become a priest. The reason for this we can only speculate about.

-:- -:- -:-

Questions for shared reflection:

(a) The conversion of St. Francis did not occur overnight, although it was initiated by imprisonment and illness. How would you compare your conversion to his?

(b) Eventually Francis was led to a life of service in the Church. To what particular service in rebuilding the Church do you feel called?

(c) In order to live the gospel Francis made some radical changes in his life-style. What changes are you ready to make in your life?

NOTES:

2

FRANCIS OUR FATHER

His Apostolic Life

Franciscans best service Christ and his Church by faithfully following the example of their father Francis. We belong to Jesus, but we look to Francis to show us how we are to live the gospel life of service.

Three Orders

The Order of Friars Minor grew rapidly as men of all classes, including clergy and nobility, humbly received the habit at Francis' hand. He required that newcomers prove their fitness by giving all their goods to the poor and ultimately serving lepers.

In 1212 with St. Clare of Assisi, who was then eighteen years of age, Francis founded his Second Order, the Poor Clares, a cloistered community of women. He installed his "Poor Ladies" in a convent built for them at his beloved church of San Damiano.

Virtually from the beginning of his preaching career (1209) crowds of devout lay people in the various towns sought his special direction in conforming their secular lives to the Gospel. Many wished to join his First or Second Order, but were bound to the world by family ties or other grave obligations. For these disciples among the laity and secular clergy Francis founded a Third Order. These secular Franciscans were given their first formal rule of life in 1221, and were already numerous throughout Italy at that time.

Missionary Efforts

Burning with zeal for souls, Francis conceived a glorious foreign missionary ideal. At a time when no one dreamed of converting Mohammedans, but only of subduing them by force of arms, he yearned to draw them to Christ, if not by his preaching, surely by shedding his blood among them. He looked upon martyrdom also as the highest degree of voluntary poverty — the spoliation of one's very life. In 1211 his first attempt to go to the Near East failed. About two years later he and a few companions journeyed to Spain en route for Morocco. But illness forced him to return to Italy.

At last, in 1219, he made his way to Egypt where he began by evangelizing the Crusaders. Daring all dangers, he strove personally to convert the arch-enemy, Sultan Malek-el-Kamel. Francis failed, but the Sultan treated him with the utmost respect, and sent him safely back to the Crusaders' camp. In 1220 news of grave crises threatening the Order in Italy obliged him to return.

That same year Francis resigned as head of the Order he had founded, appointing in his place as minister general Peter Cataneo. He had also obtained from Pope Honorius III the devoted services of Cardinal Hugolino, his close friend and collaborator, as Cardinal Protector and Corrector of his three Orders.

An Inspiration To All

His life of prayer, charity, and penance against the background of a most austere imitation of the poverty of Christ and the Blessed Virgin, continued to astound his contemporaries, who saw in him "another Jesus Christ."

He drew to himself even the birds of the air and the beasts of the forest. The original sources of his life are filled with accounts of his affection for all creatures, living and non-living, and the marvelous power he exerted over them. But the finest of all tributes to the wondrous intuition he had of the Creator's goodness as displayed in his handiwork, is Francis' own *Canticle of Brother Sun.* This radiant hymn reveals the Little Poor Man not only as a great poet, but as the patron saint of the environment or ecology.

In the year 1223 the holy founder wrote his definitive Rule for the Friars Minor. It was solemnly confirmed by Pope Honorius III, and has guided and sanctified the First Order down to the present day.

His Sufferings

The following year, September 1224, his life-long yearning to identify himself with the Savior on the cross was startlingly fulfilled. While spending forty days in fasting and prayer on Mount La Verna in Tuscany, Francis received the Sacred Stigmata. Absorbed in prayer on a cliff overlooking the beautiful Arno Valley, a crucified Seraph appeared and pierced his hands, feet, and side with wounds like those of Our Lord. Back at the Portiuncula, despite his efforts to hide the holy wounds, several of the friars managed to see and touch them.

To the sufferings of the Stigmata were added those of other infirmities, old and new, which increased from day to day. His wonderful patience and the sweetness of his disposition, together with the affection shown him by his brethren, make these last two years perhaps the most beautiful pages of his life. His sufferings, however, which he called his "sisters," stifled none of his zeal for souls. Unable to walk because of the wounds in his feet, he had himself mounted on an ass. Then, led through the towns and countryside, he continued to preach. People along the way wept, since he seemed so much like Jesus being carried about on his cross.

His Death

In the year of his death, 1226, he dictated his testament, the beautiful document in which he holds up to his friars for the last time the splendid ideal of gospel life to which the "Most High" had called him, and to which he had been faithful to the end.

Finally, almost blind and wracked by alarming symptoms of grave diseases, he had himself conveyed to his "Little

Portion," the sanctuary of Our Lady of the Angels, so dear to him because of his indescribable devotion to Mary, and because it was the cradle of the Order, the hallowed place where he had espoused Lady Poverty twenty years before.

Loyal to his Lady Poverty to the very last, he had himself laid naked on the ground. Urged by his superior, he allowed himself to be clothed again in his habit. Then, recalling the Last Supper, he blessed a loaf of bread and distributed it to his disciples. He passed a few more days in the intimacy of their company, singing with them the *Canticle of Brother Sun,* to which he added a strophe in honor of "our Sister Death."

On Saturday evening, October 3, 1226, he again had himself laid on the bare earth. While one of the brethren, at his request, was reading the thirteenth chapter of the Gospel of St. John, Francis gladly gave up his soul to God. The great heart had finally broken, but not, as Chesterton says, "until it held the world."

Two years later his friend Cardinal Hugolino, now Pope Gregory IX, canonized St. Francis of Assisi, and extended his feast to the Universal Church. The Little Poor Man became "the saint of the whole world."

-:- -:- -:-

Questions for shared reflection:

(a) The many dimensions of Francis' spirit must be considered together, always in relationship to one another. Yet what characteristic of St. Francis or event in his life touched you most personally?

(b) St. Francis had special love for his Lady Poverty, as his companion on his apostolic journeyings. Are you afraid to be poor?

(c) St. Francis suffered many physical difficulties, yet his apostolic spirit did not abate. What trials common to all of us can be more discouraging than bodily sufferings?

NOTES:

3

FROM THE STEPS OF SAINT PETER'S

The Nature and Purpose of the Order

The Secular Order of Saint Francis, like all Orders, is approved to further the redemptive work of Christ within his Church. Hence, our apostolic journey begins in Rome, from the center of the Church's world presence.

The Word of God

On the evening of that first day of the week, even though the disciples had locked the doors of the place where they were for fear of the Jews, Jesus came and stood before them. "Peace be with you," he said. When he had said this, he showed them his hands and his side. At the sight of the Lord the disciples rejoiced. "Peace be with you," he said again. "As the Father has sent me, so I send you."

—*John 20:19-21*

The eleven disciples made their way to Galilee, to the mountain to which Jesus had summoned them. At the sight of him, those who had entertained doubts fell down in homage. Jesus came forward and addressed them in these words: "Full authority has been given to me both in heaven and on earth; go, therefore, and make disciples of all the nations. Baptize them in the name 'of the Father, and of the Son, and of the Holy Spirit.' Teach them to carry out everything I have commanded you. And know that I am with you always, until the end of the world."

—*Matthew 28:16-20*

Also: Jn 21:15-19 (Peter the Shepherd); Ac 2:1-47 (descent of the Holy Spirit); IICr 10:1-18 (Paul defends his ministry); Gl 1:11-24 (called by Christ).

The Church Speaks

The Church, endowed with the gifts of her founder and faithfully observing his precepts of charity, humility, and self-denial, receives the mission of proclaiming and establishing among all peoples the kingdom of Christ and of God, and she is, on earth, the seed and the beginning of that kingdom.

—*Constitution on the Church, 5.*

Jesus Christ, the eternal pastor, set up the holy Church by entrusting the apostles with their mission as he himself had been sent by the Father. He willed that their successors, the bishops namely, should be the shepherds in his Church until the end of the world. In order that the episcopate itself, however, might be one and undivided he put Peter at the head of the other apostles, and in him he set up a lasting and visible source and foundation of the unity both of faith and of communion. This teaching concerning the institution, the permanence, the nature and import of the sacred primacy of the Roman Pontiff and his infallible teaching office, the sacred synod proposes anew to be firmly believed by all the faithful, and, proceeding undeviatingly with this same undertaking, it proposes to proclaim publicly and enunciate clearly the doctrine concerning bishops, successors of the apostles, who together with Peter's successor, the Vicar of Christ and the visible head of the whole Church, direct the house of the living God.

—*Constitution on the Church, 18.*

Also: Ap 4; Bs 4; Ch 5-7, 18-24, 32, 40, 43; Rl 8.

Franciscan Focus

Since the Church has approved the Secular Franciscan Order and ratified its Rule as an approved way of life, we go forth conscious that in all things we are sent by the Church to further Christ's work of redemption. Therefore, the Order belongs to the Church, not to St. Francis, and certainly not to Franciscans themselves.

We must never lose sight of the reason for our Order's existence. We are committed to the salvation of all through the Church, yet with a spirit that distinguishes us from other Orders. The Secular Franciscan Order provides a way of life for lay men and women (also diocesan priests) according to a Rule approved by the Church. Those called to this Order surrender themselves to Christ by promising to live the gospel life according to the example of St. Francis of Assisi.

To be admitted into the Order a candidate must be of tried fidelity in the practice of the Catholic faith and in absolute loyalty to the Roman Church and the Apostolic See. Of paramount importance is the intention to strive for Christian perfection within a secular state of life and to dedicate oneself to God in special service within the Church.

The Order is not simply a pious association of good people, nor a service organization that is part of the parish or diocese. It is a committed way of life. Secular Franciscans are Christian apostles sent by the Church into secular society as a leaven of gospel living. Since the Church gives this responsibility to many others, we must justify our existence as a separate Order by permeating our methods and attitudes with the spirit of St. Francis of Assisi.

Our Heritage

When Blessed Francis saw that the Lord God was daily adding to the number of his followers, he wrote for himself and his brothers, present and to come, simply and with few words, a form of life and rule, using for the most part the words of the holy Gospel, for the perfection of which alone he yearned. But he did insert a few other things that were necessary to provide for a holy way of life. He then came to Rome with all the aforementioned brothers, desiring very much that what he had written should be confirmed by the Lord Pope Innocent III.

—*I Celano 32. Omnibus, p. 254*

Many of the people, nobles and commoners alike, were touched by divine inspiration and began to imitate Francis' way of life, and to follow in his steps. They abandoned the cares and pomps of the world, desiring to live under his direction, guidance, and discipline.

— *Three Companions 54. Omnibus, p. 937*

Not only men, but also women and unmarried virgins were fired by the brothers' preaching, and, on their advice, entered the prescribed convents to do penance. . . . Married men and women, being bound by the marriage vow, were advised by the friars to dedicate themselves to a life of penance in their own homes.

Thus through blessed Francis' perfect devotion to the Blessed Trinity the Church of Christ was renewed by three new orders. . . . His three distinct orders were each in due time approved and confirmed by the sovereign pontiff.

— *Three Companions 60. Omnibus, p. 943*

Also: Mj II 1-8 (640); 3C 46-53 (932).

The Secular Franciscan Rule

1. The Franciscan family, as one among many spiritual families raised up by the Holy Spirit in the Church, unites all members of the People of God — laity, religious, and priests — who recognize that they are called to follow Christ in the footsteps of St. Francis of Assisi.

In various ways and forms but in life-giving union with each other, they intend to make present the charism of their common Seraphic Father in the life and mission of the Church.

2. The Secular Franciscan Order holds a special place in this family circle. It is an organic union of all Catholic fraternities scattered throughout the world and open to every group of the faithful. In these fraternities the brothers and sisters, led by the Spirit, strive for perfect charity in their own secular state. By their profession they pledge themselves to live the gospel in the manner of St. Francis by means of this rule approved by the Church.

3. The present rule, succeeding *Memoriale Propositi* (1221) and the rules approved by the Supreme Pontiffs Nicholas IV and Leo XIII, adapts the Secular Franciscan

Order to the needs and expectation of the Holy Church in the conditions of changing times. Its interpretation belongs to the Holy See and its application will be made by the General Constitutions and particular statutes.

-:- -:- -:-

Questions for shared reflection:

(a) Secular Franciscans are not only good Christians who attend Mass, receive the sacraments and obey the commandments, but are missionary Christians. In what way do you feel you qualify as a missionary?

(b) In addition to the Franciscan way of life, the Church has also approved the Dominican way of life, the Carmelite way of life, the Jesuit way of life, and others. Why do you feel you have a Franciscan "soul"?

(c) The Franciscan Order belongs to the whole Church and must support its entire mission. What areas of the Church's life are you not wholly committed to?

NOTES:

4

SIDE BY SIDE

Community Life

All Christians, by reason of their baptism, are one with each other in Jesus. The Franciscan way of life reflects this unity in a special form. Therefore, no one can follow Christ with Francis and in his spirit except in the company of other Franciscans.

The Word of God

This is my commandment: love one another as I have loved you. There is no greater love than this: to lay down one's life for one's friends. You are my friends if you do what I command you. I no longer speak of you as slaves, for a slave does not know what his master is about. Instead, I call you friends, since I have made known to you all that I heard from my Father. It was not you who chose me, it was I who chose you to go forth and bear fruit. Your fruit must endure, so that all you ask the Father in my name he will give you. The command I give you is this, that you love one another.

—*John 15:12-17*

I plead with you, then, as a prisoner for the Lord, to live a life worthy of the calling you have received, with perfect humility, meekness, and patience, bearing with one another lovingly. Make every effort to preserve the unity which has the Spirit as its origin and peace as its binding force. There is but one body and one spirit, just as there is but one hope given all of you by your call. There is one

Lord, one faith, one baptism; one God and Father of all, who is over all, and works through all, and is in all.

—*Ephesians 4:1-6*

Also: Jn 17:1-26 (Jesus' prayer for the disciples); ICr 1212-31 (analogy of the body); IJn 4:7-21 (God's love and ours).

The Church Speaks

In the human nature united to himself, the Son of God, by overcoming death through his own death and resurrection, redeemed man and changed him into a new creation. For by communicating his Spirit, Christ mystically constitutes as his body those brothers of his who are called together from every nation.

In that body the life of Christ is communicated to those who believe and who, through the sacraments, are united in a hidden and real way to Christ in his passion and glorification. Through baptism we are formed in the likeness of Christ: "For in one Spirit we were all baptized into one body" (I Cor 12:13).

—*Constitution on the Church, 7*

Gathered together in the People of God and established in the one Body of Christ under one head, the laity — no matter who they are — have, as living members, the vocation of applying to the building up of the Church and to its continual sanctification all the powers which they have received from the goodness of the Creator and from the grace of the Redeemer.

—*Constitution on the Church, 33*

Also: MW 23-25, 74.

Franciscan Focus

Francis of Assisi saw that the Son of God, by becoming our brother and sharing our mortal condition, sanctified every human relationship. He considered all creatures, especially man, in a universal brotherhood under the care of an all-loving Father. So he reached out to everyone as his brother or sister. This was to become very evident among his followers, who were to be a sign of fraternal charity.

He himself always had at least one of his brothers with him wherever he went.

Therefore, Secular Franciscans too are associated with each other in community life. Together with their brothers and/or sisters they support each other in their common calling. This is not only necessary as an expression of their oneness in Christ, but keeps in focus the purpose of a Franciscan vocation: to rebuild the Body of Christ, his Church.

Members of the Secular Franciscan Order are joined in communities (fraternities) even though they live apart from one another in their own homes. In addition to coming together in a reunion of the community at least once each month, they aid one another at all times in their needs and, when possible, cooperate in works of charity and in the apostolate of the Church.

It is impossible to be a Christian alone; it is equally impossible to follow St. Francis all by oneself.

Our Heritage

"Our order," Francis said, "is a very great company, . . . which has come together from every part of the world to live under one form of life. In it the wise turn to their own advantage what is characteristic of the simple, when they see the illiterate are seeking heavenly things with burning zeal and those who have not been taught by men learning to savor spiritual things through the Holy Spirit. In it also the simple turn to their own benefit the things that are proper to the wise, when they see renowned men who could live in glory everywhere in the world humbled in the same way as they themselves." This, he said, "is what makes the beauty of this family shine forth, whose many different ornaments please the father of the family not a little."

—II Celano 192. Omnibus, p. 516

The saint raised his hands to heaven and praised his Christ. . . . Indeed, that he might show himself to be a true imitator of Christ his God in all things, he loved to the end his brothers and sons whom he had loved from the beginning. He had all the brothers present there called to him and soothing them with comforting words in view of his death, he exhorted them with paternal affection to love God.

—II Celano 216. Omnibus, p. 535

Since the strength of Francis' love made him a brother to all creatures, it is not surprising that the charity of Christ made him more than a brother to those who are stamped with the image of their Creator. . . . He loved his brothers beyond measure with an affection that rose from his innermost being, because they were of the same household of faith and united by participation in an eternal inheritance according to the promise.

—II Celano 172. Omnibus, p. 500

Also: 3C 41-45 (928).

The Secular Franciscan Rule

13. As the Father sees in every person the features of his Son, the firstborn of many brothers and sisters, so the Secular Franciscans with a gentle and courteous spirit accept all people as a gift of the Lord and an image of Christ.

A sense of community will make them joyful and ready to place themselves on an equal with all people, especially with the lowly for whom they shall strive to create conditions of life worthy of people redeemed by Christ.

22. The local fraternity is to be established canonically. It becomes the basic unit of the whole Order and a visible sign of the Church, the community of love. This should be the privileged place for developing a sense of Church and the Franciscan vocation and for enlivening the apostolic life of its members.

-:- -:- -:-

Questions for shared reflection:

(a) What other groups of Christians do you meet with on a regular basis?

(b) What gifts of mind, body or spirit can you contribute to your Franciscan community?

(c) What support do you expect from your Franciscan brothers and sisters?

NOTES:

5

IN THE SPIRIT OF ST. FRANCIS OF ASSISI

Our Call to Holiness

To know Jesus as Francis knew him is the Franciscan spirit. We must identify with Jesus as he fulfilled the will of his Father, especially in his poverty and humility. The procedure outlined in the Secular Franciscan Rule is our path to Christian perfection.

The Word of God

Because you are God's chosen ones, holy and beloved, clothe yourselves with heartfelt mercy, with kindness, humility, meekness, and patience. Bear with one another; forgive whatever grievances you have against one another. Forgive as the Lord has forgiven you. Over all these virtues put on love, which binds the rest together and makes them perfect.

— *Colossians 3:12-15*

Praised be the God and Father of our Lord Jesus Christ, who has bestowed on us in Christ every spiritual blessing in the heavens! God chose us in him before the world began, to be holy and blameless in his sight, to be full of love; he likewise predestined us through Christ Jesus to be his adopted sons — such was his will and pleasure — that all might praise the glorious favor he has bestowed on us in his beloved.

— *Ephesians 1:3-6*

You must lay aside your former way of life and the old self which deteriorates through illusion and desire, and acquire a fresh spiritual way of thinking. You must put on that new man created in God's image, whose justice and holiness are born of truth.

—*Ephesians 4:22-24*

Also: Mt 5:3-12 (the beatitudes); Mt 5:43-48 (love of enemies); Mk 12:28-34 (the great commandment); Lk 6: 27-38 (love of one's enemies).

The Church Speaks

The followers of Christ, called by God not in virtue of their works, but by his design and grace, and justified in the Lord Jesus, have been made sons of God in the baptism of faith and partakers of the divine nature, and so are truly sanctified. They must therefore hold on to and perfect in their lives that sanctification which they have received from God. . . .

It is quite clear that all Christians in any state or walk of life are called to the fullness of Christian life and to the perfection of love, and by this holiness a more human manner of life is fostered also in earthly society. In order to reach this perfection the faithful should use the strength dealt out to them by Christ's gift, so that, following in his footsteps and conformed to his image, doing the will of God in everything, they may wholeheartedly devote themselves to the glory of God and to the service of their neighbor.

—*Constitution on the Church, 40*

Also: Ch 42.

Franciscan Focus

The Secular Franciscan way of life is contained in chapter two of the Rule.

Articles four to eight show that the Franciscan vocation is firmly based on our union with Christ and his Church.

4. We must live the Gospel of our Lord Jesus Christ.
5. We must encounter Christ in our brothers and sisters, in Sacred Scripture, in His Church and her liturgical action.
6. We must be instruments of the Church's mission of proclaiming Christ, in full communion with the pope, bishops, and priests.

7. We must prepare ourselves for this service by a life of penance, i.e., a continuing radical interior change of heart, or conversion.
8. We must let prayer and contemplation be the soul of all we are and do, and participate in the Church's sacramental life, particularly the Eucharist, and in her liturgical prayer.

Articles nine to fourteen reveal the specific Franciscan dimension of our Christian life.

9. Our life is one with Mary, the Mother of Jesus, as our first example of living with Christ.
10. Our life is one of surrender to the Father's will for us, in following the obedience of Jesus in poverty and suffering.
11. Our life is one of simplicity and humility, avoiding all show of possession and power in order to identify with Christ's own life-style.
12. Our life is one of purity, so our hearts will be free to love even the most repulsive of our brothers and sisters redeemed by Christ.
13. Our life is one of involvement, with a sense of the community of all people, especially to share, as Christ did, the human condition of the poor in their physical or spiritual deprivation.
14. Our life is one of service, using our time and energies for the good of others, not for any recompense other than to be as Jesus, who came "not to be served, but to serve."

Articles fifteen to nineteen indicate the specific apostolic service required of Franciscans.

15. We are called to lead in the promotion of justice in society by courageous initiatives.
16. We are called to show work as a service of the human community and a sharing in creation and our redemption.
17. We are called in our family life to be a sign of Christ's love for his Church, giving our neighbors an example

of peace, fidelity to God, and a respect for life as a gift from God.

18. We are called to treat all creatures, animate and inanimate, as an expression of God's goodness and with a reciprocal kinship.
19. We are called to be instruments of God's peace, bringing joy and hope by open and fraternal harmony with all.

Our Heritage

He (Francis) withdrew from the busy life of his trade and begged God in his goodness to show him what he should do. He prayed constantly until he was consumed with a passionate longing for God and was ready to give up the whole world in his desire for his heavenly home and think nothing of it. He realized that he had discovered the treasure hidden in the field and like the wise trader in the Gospel he could think of nothing but how he might sell all that he had and buy the pearl he had found. He still did not know how to go about it, but at the same tim he was forced to conclude that a spiritual venture could only begin by rejecting the world and that victory over himself would mark the beginning of his service of Christ.

—Major Life I, 4. Omnibus, p. 638

Carried away by the force of his (Francis') preaching, great numbers of people adopted the new rule of penance according to the form instituted by St. Francis which he called the "Order of the Brothers of Penance." The way of penance is common to all those who are on the road to heaven and so this way of life includes members of both sexes, clerics and layfolk, married and single.

—Major Life IV, 6. Omnibus, p. 657

Also: IC 6 (233); PV (132); TO (165); MP 27-38 (1154).

The Secular Franciscan Rule

From the Prologue: All who love the Lord with their whole heart, with their whole soul and mind, with all their strength (cf. Mk 12:30), and love their neighbors as themselves (cf. Mt 22:39) and hate their bodies with their vices and sins, and receive the Body and Blood of our Lord Jesus Christ, and produce worthy fruits of penance:

Oh, how happy and blessed are these men and women when they do these things and persevere in doing them, because "the spirit of the Lord will rest upon them" (cf. Is 11:2) and he will make "his home and dwelling among them" (cf. Jn 14:23), and they are the sons of the heavenly Father (cf. Mt 5:45), whose works they do, and they are the spouses, brothers, and mothers of our Lord Jesus Christ (cf. Mt 12:50).

We are spouses, when by the Holy Spirit the faithful soul is united with our Lord Jesus Christ, we are brothers to him when we fulfill "the will of the Father who is in heaven" (cf. Mt 12:50).

We are mothers, when we carry him in our heart and body (cf. I Cor 6:20) through divine love and a pure and sincere conscience; we give birth to him through a holy life which must give light to others by example (cf. Mt 5:16).

-:- -:- -:-

Questions for shared reflection:

(a) How do you see Franciscans as different from all other Christians?

(b) Why do you feel drawn to the Franciscan way of life rather than to some other secular order?

(c) Do you feel you have a Franciscan spirit even before you join the Order? If so, then why join?

NOTES:

6

WITHIN THE GATES OF ASSISI

The Period of Formation

A vocation to be a Secular Franciscan comes from God and is a call to fulfill a special service in the Church. It is a development of the basic Christian vocation begun at baptism. Those who feel called to this way of life must be sure that it is God's will for them, and they must be trained to fulfill its commitments. Hence, before professing the Rule of the Order, candidates or novices must spend at least one year in preparation and on probation.

The Word of God

Jesus gave him (Nicodemus) this answer: "I solemnly assure you, no one can see the reign of God unless he is begotten from above." "How can a man be born again once he is old?" retorted Nicodemus. "Can he return to his mother's womb and be born over again?" Jesus replied: "I solemnly assure you, no one can enter into God's kingdom without being begotten of water and Spirit. Flesh begets flesh; Spirit begets spirit. Do not be surprised that I tell you, you must all be begotten from above. The wind blows where it will. You hear the sound it makes, but you do not know where it comes from, or where it goes. So it is with everyone begotten of the Spirit."

—*John 3:3-8*

As he made his way along the Sea of Galilee, he observed Simon and his brother Andrew casting their nets into the sea; they were fishermen. Jesus said to them, "Come after me: I will make you fishers of men." They immediately abandoned their nets and became his followers. Proceeding a little farther along, he caught sight of James, Zebedee's son, and his brother John. They too were in their boat putting their nets in order. He summoned them on the spot. They abandoned their father Zebedee, who was in the boat with the hired men, and went off in his company.

—*Mark 1:16-20*

Another time a man came up to him and said, "Teacher, what good must I do to possess everlasting life?" He answered, ". . . If you wish to enter into life, keep the commandments." . . . The young man said to him, "I have kept all these; what do I need to do further?" Jesus told him, "If you seek perfection, go, sell your possessions, and give to the poor. You will have treasure in heaven. Afterward, come back and follow me." Hearing these words, the young man went away sad, for his possessions were many.

—*Matthew 19:16-22*

Also: ICr 15:9-10 ("I am the least of the apostles.")

The Church Speaks

While it is true that secular institutes are not religious institutes, at the same time they involve a true and full profession of the evangelical counsels in the world, recognized by the Church. This profession confers a consecration on people living in the world, men and women, laymen and clerics. Therefore they should make it their chief aim to give themselves to God totally in perfect charity. The institutes themselves ought to preserve their own special character — their secular character, that is to say — to the end that they may be able to carry on effectively and everywhere the apostolate in the world and, as it were, from the world, for which they were founded.

Let them know quite clearly, at the same time, that they will be unable to accomplish so great a task unless the members have so thorough a grounding in matters divine and human that they will be truly leaven in the world, for the strengthening and increase of the Body of Christ. Superiors therefore should devote great care to the formation, especially the spiritual formation, of their subjects, and also to the promotion of their higher studies.

—*Decree on the Renewal of Religious Life, 11*

Franciscan Focus

A simple ceremony of investiture marks the beginning of the period of formation. The habit of the Order, or Franciscan sign, is that prescribed by the 1957 General Constitutions of the Franciscan Third Order, namely, a small scapular and cord. As the Rule indicates, the sign may be different when a new General Constitutions and the particular statutes for the United States are promulgated by the Holy See.

The scapular and cord, worn under the outer clothing as garments of penance, are symbolic of the habit worn by St. Francis, a simple tunic and rope. They are a reminder that one has undertaken a new form of the Christian life, one that focuses on the poverty and humility of the Son of God.

During the period of formation the candidate, known as a novice, is under the guidance of a professed member of the council, called a novice master/mistress, who trains the novice in the virtues and in community life. In addition, the novice attends instructions on the Rule conducted by an instructor of candidates. Additional programs to foster the spiritual and intellectual growth of the candidate may be required by a particular fraternity.

The novice lives fully the life of a Secular Franciscan. This is necessary so that the full implication of a life-long commitment will be appreciated. However, the novice may leave the Order on his/her own initiative at any time before profession, or be dismissed for lack of diligence in the pursuit of the spirit of St. Francis.

The candidate's decision to make profession of the Rule is a momentous one, and can only be conscientiously arrived at through prayer, and through continuing meditation on the four Gospels (Matthew, Mark, Luke, and John). The novice at the same time, is fulfilling the daily exercises of the professed, namely, daily Mass if possible, and the recitation of the Divine Office. The Seraphic Office of the Our Father,

Hail Mary, and Glory said twelve times is rooted in tradition, but it is recommended that one of the offices commonly used in the Church today be substituted. These are: the Little Office of the Blessed Virgin Mary, or the Prayer of Christians, or the Liturgy of the Hours. Only in prayer will the novice truly discern the will of God.

Although one year is the prescribed time for the period of formation, it is considered only a minimum. The candidate can expect the time to be extended until full preparation for a permanent commitment has been realized, in the judgment of the fraternity leadership.

Our Heritage

Until the work of restoring the church of San Damiano was completed, blessed Francis still wore the garments of a hermit with a strap to serve as a belt, and he carried a staff and had sandals on his feet. Then, one day during the celebration of Mass he heard the words in which Christ bade his disciples go out and preach, carrying neither gold nor silver, nor haversack for the journey, without staff, bread, or shoes, and having no second garment. After listening to the priest's explanation of these words of the Gospel, full of unspeakable joy, he exclaimed: "This is what my whole heart desires to accomplish."

He learned these words by heart, meditating on what he had heard; and joyfully he started to put them into practice. He discarded his second garment, and from that day onwards he used no staff, shoes, or haversack; he kept one miserable tunic, and instead of the strap took a length of cord as a belt. He set his whole heart and mind on how he could best carry out the words of grace that he had heard.

—*Legend of the Three Companions, 25. Omnibus, p. 915*

By divine inspiration Francis now began to strive after Gospel perfection, inviting others also to lead a life of penance. His words were full of the power of the Holy Spirit, never empty or ridiculous, and they went straight to the heart, so that his hearers were amazed. . . . As the force of his teaching and the sincerity of his life became known, others were moved by his example to live a life of penance. They renounced everything they had and came to share his life and dress.

—*Major Life 2, 3. Omnibus, p. 647*

Also: IC 22 (247).

The Secular Franciscan Rule

23. Requests for admission to the Secular Franciscan Order must be presented to the local fraternity, whose council decides upon the acceptance of new brothers and sisters.

Admission into the Order is gradually attained through a time of initiation, a period of formation of at least one year, and profession of the rule. The entire community is engaged in this process of growth by its own manner of living. The age for profession and the distinctive Franciscan sign are regulated by the statutes.

-:- -:- -:-

Questions for shared reflection:

The period of formation is a time of testing and training as well as a time for learning:

(a) What changes will you have to make in your daily or weekly routine?

(b) What weaknesses in your spiritual character need strengthening?

(c) What aspects of your life must be eliminated or needs to be modified in order to become a follower of St. Francis?

NOTES:

II
INSTRUCTIONS FOR NOVICES
From Assisi to Everywhere

The town of Assisi, about 90 miles northeast of Rome is the birthplace of St. Francis, and here the Order began. So in *Our Journey with Jesus and Francis* we stop for a time at this place which even today is permeated with the spirit of the saint. We need to absorb his simplicity, humility, and poverty, for these underlie his way of life, and his Rule, which is studied during the period of formation, or the novitiate.

Among the first Secular Franciscans were Blessed Luchesius and his wife, Bonadonna. The way of life Francis outlined for them and the others is embodied in his *Letter to All the Faithful* (1215) and a shorter, earlier version of this *Letter*, addressed to "the Brothers and Sisters of Penance," which now forms the *Prologue* of the new rule of the Secular Franciscans. In 1221 Pope Honorius III gave official approbation to a rule for the Third Order of St. Francis, beginning with the words, *Memoriale propositi*. To this rule fraternities in various localities, e.g. Capestrano, Venice, Koenigsberg, added statutes of their own. Copies of such rules and statutes are still extant.

Two of the early Franciscan penitents were members of royalty, Queen Elizabeth of Hungary (died 1230) and King Louis IX of Francis (died 1270). They practiced the spirit of poverty and simplicity, using their wealth and power for the service of their poor and suffering subjects, to such a heroic degree that both are canonized saints and have been declared the patrons of the Franciscan Third Order.

Pope Nicholas IV in 1289 gave papal approval to a common and stable rule for the Franciscan penitents, a revision of the rule of 1221. This rule remained in effect until Pope Leo XIII in 1883 issued a new rule. The Third Order of St. Francis became the Secular Franciscan Order when the third rule was issued by Pope Paul VI on June 24, 1978.

The following twelve instructions for novices follow the order of the new rule.

1

THE WORD OF GOD SHOWS THE WAY

The Gospel Life

The Franciscan way of life, our pilgrimage to the Father, is the following of Christ in the footsteps of St. Francis of Assisi. Francis imitated Jesus according to the example of his life on earth. It is necessary, therefore, to know Jesus as he is revealed by the four evangelists.

The Word of God

On one occasion Jesus spoke thus: "Father, Lord of heaven and earth, to you I offer praise; for what you have hidden from the learned and the clever you have revealed to the merest children. Father, it is true. You have graciously willed it so. Everything has been given to me by my Father. No one knows the Son but the Father, and no one knows the Father but the Son — and anyone to whom the Son wishes to reveal him.

"Come to me, all you who are weary and find life burdensome, and I will refresh you. Take my yoke upon your shoulders and learn from me, for I am gentle and humble of heart. Your souls will find rest, for my yoke is easy and my burden light."

—*Matthew 11:25-30*

But those things I used to consider gain I have now reappraised as loss in the light of Christ. I have come to rate all as loss in the light of the surpassing knowledge of my Lord Jesus Christ.

—*Phillipians 3:7-8*

After he had washed their feet, he put his cloak back on and reclined at table once more. He said to them: "Do you understand what I just did for you? You address me as 'Teacher' and 'Lord,' and fittingly enough, for that is what I am. But if I washed your feet — I who am Teacher and Lord — then you must wash each other's feet. What I just did was to give you an example: as I have done, so you must do. I solemnly assure you, no slave is greater than his master; no messenger outranks the one who sent him. Once you know all these things, blest will you be if you put them into practice."

—*John 13:12-17*

Also: Jn 3:16 (Nicodemus); Jn 5:19-30 (authority of the Son); Jn 10:1-18 (Good Shepherd); Jn 14:6 ("I am the way . . ."); Cl 1:15-20 (Image of the Invisible God).

The Church Speaks

It is common knowledge that among all the inspired writings, even among those of the New Testament, the Gospels have a special place, and rightly so, because they are our principal source for the life and teaching of the Incarnate Word, our Savior.

The Church has always and everywhere maintained, and continues to maintain, the apostolic origin of the four Gospels. The apostles preached, as Christ had charged them to do, and then, under the inspiration of the Holy Spirit, they and others of the apostolic age handed on to us in writing the same message they had preached, the foundation of our faith: the fourfold Gospel, according to Matthew, Mark, Luke and John.

—*Decree on Divine Revelation, 18*

Only the light of faith and meditation on the Word of God can enable us to find everywhere and always the God "in whom we live and exist" (Acts 17:28); only thus can we seek his will in everything, see Christ in all men, acquaintance or stranger, make sound judgments on the true meaning and value of temporal realities both in themselves and in relation to man's end.

Those with such a faith live in the hope of the revelation of the sons of God, keeping in mind the cross and resurrection of the Lord.

The Gospel Life

On life's pilgrimage they are hidden with Christ in God, are free from the slavery of riches, are in search of the goods that last for ever. Generously they exert all their energies in extending God's kingdom, in making the Christian spirit a vital energizing force in the temporal sphere. In life's trials they draw courage from hope, "convinced that present sufferings are no measure of the future glory to be revealed in us" (Rom. 8:18).

—*Decree on the Apostolate of the Laity, 4*

Also: Ap 30.

Franciscan Focus

St. Francis was thrilled with the thought that God our Father loved us so much that He sent his only-begotten Son to be our brother, to share our life, and then to die for our redemption. He wished to imitate the example of Christ in as full a human expression as possible. Hence, the Gospel as the revelation of Christ's life and words was his constant guide on his journey with Jesus.

Secular Franciscans, as indeed all Christians, are to live Christ's life in this world. But followers of St. Francis seek to do more. Since their life-style is to reflect the poverty and humility of the Son of God, ever ready to share his sufferings, they must be totally immersed in the Good News. We cannot imitate Jesus in his life on earth unless we thoroughly know and appreciate his words and deeds.

It is not just a matter of studying and knowing what is in the Gospels. More importantly, they must become the basis of our prayer and meditation. This should be our daily practice, and for longer periods on Sundays and feastdays. We need to read and pray the Gospel as a personal instruction from Jesus himself. Then, armed with his word and example, we go forth into the world, to return again for more understanding, "going from gospel to life and life to the gospel."

Our Heritage

Francis' highest intention, his chief desire, his uppermost purpose was to observe the holy Gospel in all things and through all things and, with perfect vigilance, with all zeal, with all the longing of his mind and all the fervor of his heart, "to follow the teaching and the footsteps of our Lord Jesus Christ." He would recall Christ's words through persistent meditation and bring to mind his deeds through the most penetrating consideration. The humility of the incarnation and the charity of the passion occupied his memory particularly, to the extent that he wanted to think of hardly anything else.

—I Celano, 84. Omnibus, p. 299

When God gave me some friars, there was no one to tell me what I should do, but the Most High himself made it clear to me that I must live the life of the Gospel.

—The Testament of St. Francis. Omnibus, p. 68

A certain Bernard of the city of Assisi . . . said to Francis: "Everything I have, I recognize as having been given me by God and at your advice I stand ready to give them back to him." "If you wish to prove what you say by deeds," the holy man said, "let us go early in the morning to the church and taking the book of the Gospel, let us seek counsel from Christ."

—II Celano, 15. Omnibus, p. 374

Also: Ic 18 (244), 110 (323), 115 (329); IIC 102-104 (446); Mj XI 1-2 (711).

The Secular Franciscan Rule

4. The rule and life of the Secular Franciscans is this: to observe the gospel of our Lord Jesus Christ by following the example of St. Francis of Assisi, who made Christ the inspiration and the center of his life with God and people.

Christ, the gift of the Father's love, is the way to him, the truth into which the Holy Spirit leads us, and the life which he has come to give abundantly.

Secular Franciscans should devote themselves especially to careful reading of the gospel, going from gospel to life and life to the gospel.

5. Secular Franciscans, therefore, should seek to encounter the living and active person of Christ in their brothers and sisters, in Sacred Scripture, in the Church, and in

liturgical activity. The faith of St. Francis, who often said "I see nothing bodily of the Most High Son of God in this world except his most holy body and blood," should be the inspiration and pattern of their eucharistic life.

-:- -:- -:-

Questions for shared reflection:

(a) Which incident in the Gospels shows you most effectively that Jesus is like us "in all things but sin," revealing that he is truly human?

(b) How often do you read the Scriptures, and what difficulties do you find in applying them to yourself?

(c) Have you ever opened the Scriptures to find out what God wanted you to do in a specific circumstance?

NOTES:

2

WITH AND THROUGH THE CHURCH

Loyalty to the Vicar of Christ

An essential difference between St. Francis and others of his day who wanted to renew the Christian life was his complete dedication to the Church as being one with Christ. They could not be separated. He believed strongly that Christ's authority to teach and guide had been given to the pope and bishops, and the holy sacraments had been entrusted to their care. He held the simplest priest, even a known sinner, in the highest respect, because it is through the priest that Christ comes to us in the Eucharist. His love for Christ was expressed by his obedience to the Church and her ministers.

The Word of God

"He who hears you, hears me. He who rejects you, rejects me. And he who rejects me, rejects him who sent me."

—*Luke 10:16*

"And you," he said to them, "who do you say that I am?" "You are the Messiah," Simon Peter answered, "the Son of the living God!" Jesus replied, "Blest are you, Simon son of Jonah! No mere man has revealed this to you, but my heavenly Father. I for my part declare to you, you are 'Rock,' and on this rock I will build my church, and the jaws of death shall not prevail against it. I will entrust to you the keys of the kingdom of heaven. Whatever you declare bound on earth shall be bound in heaven; whatever you declare loosed on earth shall be loosed in heaven."

"I am the true vine and my Father is the vinegrower.

He prunes away every barren branch, but the fruitful ones he trims clean to increase their yield. You are clean already, thanks to the word I have spoken to you. Live on in me, as I do in you. No more than a branch can bear fruit of itself apart from the vine, can you bear fruit apart from me. I am the vine, you are the branches. He who lives in me and I in him, will produce abundantly, for apart from me you can do nothing."

—John 15:1-15

Also: ICr 4:1-5 (Christ judges his ministers.)

The Church Speaks

In the Church there is diversity of ministry but unity of mission. To the apostles and their successors Christ has entrusted the office of teaching, sanctifying and governing in his name and by his power. But the laity are made to share in the priestly, prophetical, and kingly office of Christ; they have therefore, in the Church and in the world, their own assignment in the mission of the whole People of God.

—Decree on the Apostolate of the Laity, 2

As all the members of the human body, though they are many, form one body, so also are the faithful in Christ (cf. I Cor. 1212). Also, in the building up of Christ's body there is engaged a diversity of members and functions. There is only one spirit who, according to his own richness and the needs of the ministries, gives his different gifts for the welfare of the Church (cf. I Cor. 12:1-11). Among these gifts the primary belongs to the grace of the apostles to whose authority the Spirit himself subjects even those who are endowed with charisms (cf. I Cor. 14).

— Constitution on the Church, 7

Also: Bs 2.

Franciscan Focus

Attempts by many at the time of St. Francis to revitalize the Christian life created great confusion in the Church, even heresy. Too many called for disobedience to the Church, citing the often scandalous conduct of many priests and some bishops. They claimed that such clergy lost the right to be obeyed or respected, and even denied their power to consecrate the Eucharist or forgive sins.

But St. Francis would have none of this. He showed by word and action that love of Christ demands loyalty and obedience to the pope and bishops, and respect for every priest. His followers, therefore, ought to be the first to show other Christians by positive action that they believe the pope to be the vicar of Christ and the bishops the successors of the Apostles, that they indeed exercise the authority of Christ. And respect for every priest would include in a special way, obedience to one's pastor as the shepherd of the local parish, since he shares in the authority of the bishop who appointed him.

In this age of renewal, following the Second Vatican Council, the Secular Franciscans must show by word and example, by creative initiative, that the Spirit moves within the Church. They must not only "stand by the pope" but be responsive to the directives of the Holy See, the bishop of the diocese, and the pastor of the parish. It would violate the Franciscan spirit to stand by and do nothing as it would to be openly disobedient and critical.

St. Francis would have us be the "servants of the Church," who reflect by their lives the obedience of Christ to the will of his Father.

Our Heritage

Francis left the town one day to meditate out-of-doors and as he was passing by the church of San Damiano, which was threatening to collapse with age, he felt urged to go in and pray. There as he knelt in prayer before a painted image of the Crucified, he felt greatly comforted in spirit and his eyes were full of tears as he gazed at the cross. Then, all of a sudden, he heard a voice coming from the cross and telling him three times, "Francis, go and repair my house. You see it is all falling down." Francis was alone in the church and he was terrified at the sound of the voice, but the power of its message penetrated his heart and he went into an ecstasy. Eventually, he came back to himself and prepared to obey the command he had received. He was quite willing to devote himself entirely to repairing the ruined church of San Damiano, although the message really referred to the universal church which Christ "won for himself at the price of his own blood" (Acts 20:28), as the Holy Spirit afterwards made him realize and he himself explained to the friars.

—*Major Life II, 1. Omnibus, p. 640*

St. Francis saw that his brothers were increasing in number and in merits, and already they were twelve men, all steadfastly set on one purpose. Therefore he, being the twelfth, said to the others: "I see, Brothers, that God in his mercy means to increase our company; let us therefore go to our holy Mother the Roman Church and lay before the Supreme Pontiff what our Lord has begun to work through us, so that with his consent and direction we may continue what we have undertaken."

—*Three Companions, 46. Omnibus, p. 932*

Francis said: "The Lord has called us to reawaken the faith and to assist the prelates and clerics of our holy Mother the Church. Likewise we are bound, to the extent possible, to love them always, to honor and venerate them."

—*Legend of Perugia, 15. Omnibus, p. 991*

Also: Ad 26 (86); IIC 25 (383), 146 (479); Mj III 8-10 (650).

The Secular Franciscan Rule

6. They have been made living members of the Church by being buried and raised with Christ in baptism; they have been united more intimately with the Church by profession. Therefore, they should go forth as witnesses and instruments of her mission among all people, proclaiming Christ by their life and words.

Called like St. Francis to rebuild the Church and inspired by his example, let them devote themselves energetically to living in full communion with the pope, bishops, and priests, fostering an open and trusting dialogue of apostolic effectiveness and creativity.

Questions for shared reflection:

(a) To what extent are you involved in the life of your parish community?

(b) Have you ever found yourself afraid or unable to defend the Church?

(c) What special contribution do you feel Franciscans should be offering the Church in this age of renewal?

NOTES:

3

IN THE EMBRACE OF JESUS CRUCIFIED

Our Life of Penance

Being aware of our sinfulness, that we have been redeemed by the suffering and death of Jesus, is the starting point toward union with God. By turning to God and living in gratitude for his mercy, our life ceases to be one of self-indulgence. As did Francis of Assisi, we draw close to Jesus on the cross, loving him in the knowledge that he hangs there for us. Our desire is to share his sufferings.

The Word of God

Jesus then said to his disciples: "If a man wishes to come after me, he must deny his very self, take up his cross, and begin to follow in my footsteps. Whoever would save his life will lose it, but whoever loses his life for my sake will find it."

—*Matthew 16:24-25*

Are you not aware that we who were baptized into Christ Jesus were baptized into his death? Through baptism into his death we were buried with him, so that, just as Christ was raised from the dead by the glory of the Father, we too might live a new life. If we have been united with him through likeness to his death, so shall we be through a like resurrection. This we know: our old self was crucified with him so that the sinful body might be destroyed and we might be slaves to sin no longer.

—*Romans 6:3-6*

When a man can suffer injustice and endure hardship through his awareness of God's presence, this is the work of grace in him. If you do wrong and get beaten for it, what credit can you claim? But if you put up with suffering for doing what is right, this is acceptable in God's eyes. It was for this you were called, since Christ suffered for you in just this way and left you an example, to have you follow in his footsteps. He did no wrong; no deceit was found in his mouth. When he was insulted, he returned no insult. When he was made to suffer, he did not counter with threats. Instead, he delivered himself up to the One who judges justly. In his own body he brought your sins to the cross, so that all of us, dead to sin, could live in accord with God's will. By his wounds you were healed.

—I Peter 2:19-24

Also: Mt 3:1-12 (John the Baptizer); Mt 26:36-66 (agony in the garden); Mk 8:34-39 (doctrine of the cross); Lk 23: 1-56 (the crucifixion); ICR 15:50-58 (glorification of the body).

The Church Speaks

In a special way also, those who are weighed down by poverty, infirmity, sickness, and other hardships should realize that they are united to Christ, who suffers for the salvation of the world; let those feel the same who suffer persecution for the sake of justice, those whom the Lord declared blessed in the Gospel and whom "the God of all grace, who has called us to his eternal glory in Christ Jesus will himself restore, establish, strengthen, and settle" (I Peter 5:10).

—Constitution on the Church, 41

Also: Lt 109-110; Ch 8; Pr 18.

Franciscan Focus

Although now called the Secular Franciscan Order, and for most of its existence the Third Order of St. Francis, in the prologue of the rule we are reminded of our origin as a penitential movement. We were called by St. Francis "The Brothers and Sisters of Penance" and after his death we were known as "The Penitents of St. Francis." Hence, penance — or a daily conversion — is the primary attitude of a Franciscan. For this we must acquire a union with Christ's passion, since penance has no meaning apart from the cross.

Sufferings and pain, fatigue and disappointments, service unrewarded, and humiliations are part of every life. All Christians should accept them patiently. St. Francis has shown us, however, that they are to be seen as opportunities to share an intimacy with Jesus in his mission of salvation.

True penance must be filled with a spirit of gratitude and joy, not of pessimism. Through the cross we will share in Christ's resurrection. And the opportunity to partake of Christ's sufferings is seen as a privilege he grants to those he loves. It is a means of making reparation for our sins, because it was for sin that Christ died.

Hence, a life of penance calls for frequent reception of the Sacrament of Reconciliation, so we can keep strong our awareness of God's mercy. It keeps us "turned toward God" (conversion) and prompts us continually to make reparation for our sins.

St. Francis so desired to experience the sufferings of Jesus and to feel the love for us which filled the heart of Jesus, that God impressed on his flesh the Holy Stigmata, that is, the five wounds Jesus received on the cross. We could desire nothing better.

Our Heritage

A short while after his conversion, as he was walking alone along the road not far from the church of St. Mary of the Portiuncula, he was uttering loud cries and lamentation as he went. And a spiritually-minded man who met him, fearing that he was suffering from some painful ailment, said to him, "What is your trouble, brother?" But he replied, "I am not ashamed to travel through the whole world in this way, bewailing the Passion of my Lord."

—Mirror of Perfection. Omnibus, p. 1226

Francis said: "And now hear the conclusion, Brother Leo. Above all the graces and gifts of the Holy Spirit which Christ gives to His friends is that of conquering oneself and willingly enduring sufferings, insults, humiliations, and hardships for the love of Christ. For we cannot glory in all those other marvelous gifts of God, as they are not ours but God's, as the Apostle says: 'What have you that you have not received?'

"But we can glory in the cross of tribulations and afflictions, because that is ours, and so the Apostle says: 'I will not glory save in the Cross of Our Lord Jesus Christ!'"

—*Little Flowers of St. Francis, 8. Omnibus, p. 1320*

The next day came, that is, the feast of the Cross. And St. Francis, sometime before dawn, began to pray outside the entrance of his cell, turning his face toward the east. And he prayed in this way: "My Lord Jesus Christ, I pray You to grant me two graces before I die: the first is that during my life I may feel in my soul and in my body, as much as possible, that pain which You, dear Jesus, sustained in the hour of Your most bitter Passion. The second is that I may feel in my heart, as much as possible, that excessive love with which You, O Son of God, were inflamed in willingly enduring such suffering for us sinners."

—*Little Flowers of St. Francis, Part II. Omnibus, p. 1448*

Also: IIC 11 (371); Mj XIV 1 (737); MP 91 (1225).

The Secular Franciscan Rule

7. United by their vocation as "brothers and sisters of penance," and motivated by the dynamic power of the gospel, let them conform their thoughts and deeds to those of Christ by means of that radical interior change which the gospel itself calls "conversion." Human frailty makes it necessary that this conversion be carried out daily.

On this road to renewal the sacrament of reconciliation is the privileged sign of the Father's mercy and the source of grace.

-:- -:- -:-

Questions for shared reflection:

(a) When you make the Stations of the Cross, a truly

Franciscan devotion, are you able to relate your own physical or emotional pain to the sufferings of Jesus?

(b) What opportunities for penance came up in your life this week?

(c) Do you think that people know when things are not going well with you on a particular day?

NOTES:

4

ALWAYS PRAISING THE FATHER

Our Life of Prayer

In our travels with Jesus we must always keep in mind that he belongs to others as well as ourselves, having been sent by his Father for the salvation of all. The Father's love for us is shown in this gift of his Son, given to us as a brother to share our human condition. Therefore, our hearts must be filled with gratitude and praise as we speak with and listen to God — Father, Son, and Holy Spirit.

The Word of God

God's love was revealed in our midst in this way: he sent his only Son to the world that we might have life through him. Love, then, consists in this: not that we have loved God but that he has loved us and sent his Son as an offering for our sins.

—I John 4:9-10

Jesus explained to them: "I myself am the bread of life. No one who comes to me shall ever be hungry, no one who believes in me shall ever thirst. But as I told you — though you have seen me, you still do not believe. All that the Father gives me shall come to me; no one who comes will I ever reject, because it is not to do my own will that I have come down from heaven, but to do the will of him who sent me."

—John 6:35-38

"Your Father knows what you need before you ask him. This is how you are to pray: 'Our Father in heaven, hallowed be your name, your kingdom come, your will be done on earth as it is in heaven. Give us today our daily bread, and forgive us the wrong we have done as we forgive those who wrong us. Subject us not to the trial but deliver us from the evil one.' "

—*Matthew 6:8-13*

Also: Mk 1:9-11 (the baptism of Jesus); Jn 5:19-30 (the work of the Son); Jn 8:25-29, 16: 4-33 (Jesus and his Father).

The Church Speaks

The Christian is indeed called to pray with others, but he must also enter into his bedroom to pray to his Father in secret; furthermore, according to the teaching of the apostle, he must pray without ceasing. We also learn from the same apostle that we must always carry around in our bodies the dying of Jesus, so that the life also of Jesus may be made manifest in our mortal flesh.

—*Constitution on the Sacred Liturgy, 12*

The discovery of intimacy with God, the necessity for adoration, the need for intercession — the experience of Christian holiness shows us the fruitfulness of prayer, in which God reveals himself to the spirit and heart of his servants. The Lord gives us this knowledge of himself in the fervor of love. The gifts of the Spirit are many, but they always grant us a taste of that true and intimate knowledge of the Lord.

—*Decree on the Renewal of Religious Life, 43*

Also: Ap 4; Rl 6-7.

Franciscan Focus

We do not grow in God's life unless we pray. We cannot find strength to do his will except from God himself. Prayer has the power to open our souls to his action within us.

In times of prayer, however, we must not separate the three Persons in God from each other, nor from all others who share the divine life. Jesus must not be loved in isolation. We are not able to live the life of Jesus Christ, to love him in and for himself, unless we share his relationship to his Father and to the Holy Spirit whom he sent. The prayer of Jesus was always "not my will but yours be done," — and in all things he glorified his heavenly Father.

This was the secret of prayer for St. Francis. He united himself with Jesus in giving praise to the Father. Through this intimacy with Jesus he came to know the will of the Father and receive the strength of the Holy Spirit. Thus in prayer he entered the life of the Blessed Trinity. His life of prayer, so simple and dircet, is summed up in the phrase Francis so often used: "My God and my All!" which is considered the motto of the Franciscan Order.

To pray with Jesus is the way to know and love the Son of God made Man. It begets a deep understanding of his life on earth, the life which Franciscans imitate.

Our personal prayer, however, flows from our unity with the entire Body of Christ, his Church — primarily in the Sacrifice of the Mass. In view of our profession before the Church, this unity is also expressed in our daily recitation of the Divine Office. Indeed, faithfulness to the Divine Office each day — an obligation of which St. Francis makes special mention in his *Testament* — can be considered a barometer of the sincerity of our Franciscan commitment.

In prayer Christ enters the very core of our daily life. Those things we call "distractions" are often the very things he must become part of, so we can ascertain the Father's will concerning them.

Prayer is a response to being loved. But love takes time; it takes surrender; it takes silence. There must be occasional times of prayer over extended periods, when we separate ourselves from the affairs of daily living. God must have a chance to speak with us in the quiet of our souls. Frequent meditation is needed; and when God sees fit, he will lift us up in contemplation.

With St. Francis certain dimensions of Christ's life became the focal points of his prayer, namely, the birth of Jesus (his poverty and humility), the agony of the passion (his sufferings), and the Eucharist (his abiding presence). Hence, all Franciscans should have special devotion to the Infant Jesus, the crucified Jesus, and Jesus in the Blessed Sacrament.

Our Heritage

Now St. Francis, as soon as he entered the room (in the home of Bernard of Quintavalle), in order to conceal the divine graces which he had, immediately threw himself down on the bed, showing that he wished to sleep. But the Lord Bernard planned to watch him secretly during the night. And he too soon lay down, and he used such cunning that after he had rested in bed a while, he pretended to be sleeping soundly, and he began to snore loudly.

Therefore, St. Francis, who faithfully concealed the secrets of God, when he thought that the Lord Bernard was fast asleep, during the first part of the night, got out of bed and began to pray. Looking up to Heaven and raising his hands, he prayed with intense fervor and devotion, saying: "My God and my All!" And he sobbed out those words with so many tears and kept repeating them with such persistence that until matins he said nothing but "My God and my All!"

—*Little Flowers of St. Francis, 2. Omnibus, p. 1303*

St. Francis realized that he was an exile from the Lord's presence as long as he was at home in the body (cf. 2 Cor 5, 6, 8), and his love of Christ had left him with no desire for the things of this earth. Therefore, he tried to keep his spirit always in the presence of God, by praying to him without intermission, so that he might not be without some comfort from his Beloved. . . .

Francis learned in his prayer that the presence of the Holy Spirit for which he longed was granted more intimately, when he was far from the rush of worldly affairs. Therefore, he used to seek out lonely places in the wilderness and go into abandoned churches to pray at night.

—*Major Life X, 1, 3. Omnibus, p. 705, 707*

Also: CS (130); OF (159); IC 45 (266); IIC 94-101 (439).

The Secular Franciscan Rule

8. As Jesus was the true worshipper of the Father, so let prayer and contemplation be the soul of all they are and do.

Questions for shared reflection:

(a) Instead of "praying without ceasing," are you often "too busy to pray"?

(b) How do you handle distractions during prayer?

(c) What balance do you strike between prayer to the Blessed Virgin Mary and the saints with prayer to God himself?

NOTES:

5

WITH THE STRENGTH OF JESUS AND HIS SACRIFICE

The Holy Eucharist

Jesus has given us his flesh to eat, strengthening us and making us one in him. Baptized into his death we are his Body the Church and our unity is most effectively signified each time we participate in offering together with him the Sacrifice of the Mass, the unbloody renewal of his death on the cross. Herein lies the vitality of our Christian life and the focus of all divine action.

The Word of God

Thereupon Jesus said to them: "Let me solemnly assure you, if you do not eat the flesh of the Son of Man and drink his blood, you have no life in you. He who feeds on my flesh and drinks my blood has life eternal, and I will raise him up on the last day. For my flesh is real food and my blood real drink. The man who feeds on my flesh and drinks my blood remains in me, and I in him. Just as the Father who has life sent me and I have life because of the Father, so the man who feeds on me will have life because of me. This is the bread that came down from heaven. Unlike your ancestors who ate and died nonetheless, the man who feeds on this bread shall live forever."

—*John 6:53-58*

I received from the Lord what I handed on to you, namely, that the Lord Jesus on the night in which he was betrayed took bread, and after he had given thanks, broke it and said, "This is my body, which is for you. Do this in remembrance of me." In the same way, after the supper, he took the cup, saying, "This cup is the new covenant in my blood. Do this, whenever you drink it, in remembrance of me." Every time, then, you eat this bread and drink this cup, you proclaim the death of the Lord until he comes!

—*I Corinthians 11:23-26*

Also: Lk 22:15-20 (The Holy Eucharist).

The Church Speaks

Taking part in the eucharistic sacrifice, the source and summit of the Christian life, they (the faithful) offer the divine victim to God and themselves along with it. And so it is that, both in the offering and in Holy Communion, each in his own way, though not of course indiscriminately, has his own part to play in the liturgical action. Then, strengthened by the body of Christ in the eucharistic communion, they manifest in a concrete way that unity of the People of God which this holy sacrament aptly signifies and admirably realizes.

—*Constitution on the Church, 11*

The liturgy is the summit toward which the activity of the Church is directed; it is also the fount from which all her power flows. For the goal of apostolic endeavor is that all who are made sons of God by faith and baptism should come together to praise God in the midst of his Church, to take part in the Sacrifice and to eat the Lord's Supper.

—*Constitution on the Sacred Liturgy, 10*

Also: Ch 42; Lt 9-10, 47-49.

Franciscan Focus

There can be no Franciscan life without the Eucharist, because the Holy Sacrifice of the Mass is the center of our Christian life and thus is the center of our Franciscan life. We participate in the Mass not as followers of Francis but as members of the Body of Christ united with the whole Church in giving praise and thanksgiving to the Father.

Francis saw the great love of Jesus for him when he looked upon the crucifix. Thus he was drawn to the Sacrament of the Body and Blood of Jesus Christ, since it is in the Eucharist, the Sacrifice of the Mass, that the death of Jesus is proclaimed. His desire to be one with the Son of God prompted his great reverence and devotion toward the corporal presence of Jesus in this world.

From his relationship to Christ in the Eucharist Francis was able to grow closer to all other Christians who shared with him the same bread from heaven and in its strength to follow Christ in the path of his earthly life.

Hence Franciscans, following the example of their Seraphic Father, give first place in their daily lives to the Mass and to Eucharistic devotion. This makes possible that intimacy with Jesus which drives them with the fervor and zeal of Francis toward the radical living of the Gospel which is their life.

Furthermore, the Eucharist does not stand apart from the other sacraments, except as the most sublime and the focal point of the Church's sacramental and liturgical life. This includes, for us, the Liturgy of the Hours — or Divine Office. Therefore, our appreciation for the Eucharist requires full participation in the liturgical life of the Church. Franciscans, as good Catholics, must be examples of active cooperation in the renewal of the liturgy, as called for by the Second Vatican Council. Christ expects it of us. The Eucharist is the sacrament of unity in his Body, the Church.

Our Heritage

No human tongue could describe the passionate love with which Francis burned for Christ, his Spouse; he seemed to be completely absorbed by the fire of divine love like a burning coal. . . .

The memory of Christ Jesus crucified was ever present in the depths of his heart like a bundle of myrrh, and he longed to be wholly transformed into him by the fire of love. . . . He loved Christ so fervently and Christ returned his love so intimately that he seemed to have his Savior before his eyes continually, as he once privately admitted to his companions. He burned with love for the Sacrament of our Lord's Body with all his heart, and was lost in wonder at the thought of such condescending love, such loving condescension. He received Holy Communion often and so devoutly that he roused others to devotion too.

—*Major Life IX, 1-2. Omnibus, p. 698*

Our whole being should be seized with fear, the whole world should tremble and heaven rejoice, when Christ the Son of the living God is present on the altar in the hands of the priest. What wonderful majesty! What stupendous condescension! O sublime humility! O humble sublimity! That the Lord of the whole universe, God and the Son of God, should humble himself like this and hide under the form of a little bread, for our salvation.

—*Letter to a General Chapter. Omnibus, p. 105*

Not to hear at least one Mass each day, if he could be there, Francis considered no small contempt. He frequently received Holy Communion, and he did so with such devotion, that he made others also devout.

—*II Celano, 201. Omnibus, p. 523*

Also: Ad 1 (77); 3C 57 (941); Pr 80 (1055); MP 65 (1191).

The Secular Franciscan Rule

8. Let them participate in the sacramental life of the Church, above all the Eucharist. Let them join in liturgical prayer in one of the forms proposed by the Church, reliving the mysteries of the life of Christ.

-:- -:- -:-

Questions for shared reflection:

(a) When you assist at Mass, to what extent are you more concerned about your personal relationship to Jesus than being one of God's People offering His sacrifice?
(b) When you grow weary in your work as an apostle of Jesus, do you seek strength "at the Master's feet," i.e., in his Eucharistic presence?
(c) Are you more than an observer at your parish's weekend Eucharistic Liturgy?

NOTES:

6

IN COMPANY WITH MARY

The Mother of Jesus

To develop a true knowledge and love of Jesus Christ, the Son of God made Man, calls for a tender devotion toward his mother, Mary. She was very much a part of his life, being with Christ in Bethlehem and Nazareth, but more importantly on Calvary. St. Francis recognized this special relationship with her Son in light of our redemption. Therefore, he bade his followers to love her as their queen and their mother.

The Word of God

In the sixth month, the angel Gabriel was sent from God to a town of Galilee named Nazareth, to a virgin betrothed to a man named Joseph, of the house of David. The virgin's name was Mary. . . . The angel went on to say to her: "Do not fear, Mary. You have found favor with God. You shall conceive and bear a son and give him the name Jesus." . . . Mary said: "I am the servant of the Lord. Let it be done to me as you say."

—*Luke 1:26-38*

The child's father and mother were marveling at what was being said about him. Simeon blessed them and said to Mary his mother: "This child is destined to be the downfall and the rise of many in Israel, a sign that will be opposed — and you yourself shall be pierced with a sword — so that the thoughts of many hearts may be laid bare."

—*Luke 2:33-35*

Near the cross of Jesus there stood his mother, his

mother's sister, Mary the wife of Clopas, and Mary Magdalene. Seeing his mother there with the disciple whom he loved, Jesus said to his mother, "Woman, there is your son." In turn he said to the disciple, "There is your mother." From that hour onward, the disciple took her into his care.

—*John 19:25-27*

Also: Lk 1:39-56 (the Visitation); Lk 2:41-52 (the finding in the temple); Jn 2:1-12 (the wedding at Cana); Ac 1:12-14 (Mary and the Apostles); Rv 12:1-6 (the woman and the dragon).

The Church Speaks

Wishing in his supreme goodness and wisdom to effect the redemption of the world, "when the fullness of time came, God sent his Son, born of a woman . . . that we might receive the adoption of sons" (Gal. 4:4). "He for us men, and for our salvation, came down from heaven, and was incarnated by the Holy Spirit from the Virgin Mary." This divine mystery of salvation is revealed to us and continued in the Church, which the Lord established as his body. Joined to Christ the head and in communion with all his saints, the faithful must in the first place reverence the memory "of the glorious ever Virgin Mary, Mother of God and of our Lord Jesus Christ."

—*Constitution on the Church, 52*

The Blessed Virgin Mary advanced in her pilgrimage of faith, and faithfully persevered in her union with her Son unto the cross, where she stood, in keeping with the divine plan, enduring with her only begotten Son the intensity of his suffering, associated herself with his sacrifice in her mother's heart, and lovingly consenting to the immolation of this victim which was born of her. Finally, she was given by the same Christ Jesus dying on the cross as a mother to his disciple, with these words: "Woman, behold thy son" (Jn 19:26-27).

—*Constitution on the Church, 58*

Perfect model of this apostolic spiritual life is the Blessed Virgin Mary, Queen of Apostles. While on earth her life was like that of any other, filled with labors and the cares of the home; always, however, she remained intimately united to her Son and cooperated in an entirely unique way in the Savior's work. And now, assumed into heaven, "her motherly love keeps her attentive to her Son's brothers, still on pilgrimage amid the dangers and difficulties of life, until they arrive at the happiness of the fatherland." Everyone should have a genuine devotion to her and entrust his life to her motherly care.

—*Decree on the Apostolate of the Laity, 4*

Also: Ap 40; Ch 53-69; Lt 103.

Franciscan Focus

Our love for Jesus includes his mother. This follows not only because Jesus loved her and would expect his followers to do so, but because she is, more than any other mother, so intimately part of his life's purpose.

St. Francis loved Mary as a devoted son. As the spouse of the Holy Spirit, she not only made Jesus, the Son of God, our brother, but Francis saw how she shared his poverty and suffering. Being our mother too, she gives her example to strengthen us in our efforts to be poor and humble servants of the Lord.

Mary is the mother of the whole Church, of all those baptized into the death of her Son. Through her union with his sufferings on Calvary, she gave birth to his Body the Church. After the Ascension she remained with the infant Church on earth to nourish it. Now in heaven she continues as its mother, but also as queen in the eternal kingdom.

And so, in like manner, Francis called her the queen and mother of his Order. He wanted her to love and protect those of her children who give her honor by serving the Church according to a life-style that reflects her Son's earthly life — and hers. Francis loved her so much because he felt that she showed him how to fulfill his desire to follow wherever Christ would lead him. She would show him how to serve the Church, to do the work of her Son.

Our Heritage

He (Francis) embraced the Mother of our Lord Jesus

with indescribable love because, as he said, it was she who made the Lord Jesus our brother, and through her we found mercy. After Christ, he put all his trust in her and took her as his patroness for himself and his friars. In her honor he fasted every year from the feast of Saints Peter and Paul until the Assumption.

—*Major Life IX, 3. Omnibus, p. 699*

As he was living there by the church of our Lady, Francis prayed to her who had conceived the Word, full of grace and truth, begging her insistently and with tears to become his Advocate. Then he was granted the true spirit of the Gospel by the intercession of the Mother of Mercy and he brought it to fruition.

—*Major Life III, 1. Omnibus, p. 646*

Toward the Mother of Jesus he was filled with an inexpressible love, because it was she who made the Lord of Majesty our brother. He sang special *Praises* to her, poured out prayers to her, offered her his affections, so many and so great that the tongue of man cannot recount them. But what delights us most, he made her the advocate of the order and placed under her wings the sons he was about to leave that she might cherish them and protect them to the end.

—*II Celano 198. Omnibus, p. 521*

Also: VM (135); IC 24 (248); Mj VIII 5 (691); 3C 15 (905); MP 55 (1177).

The Secular Franciscan Rule

9. The Virgin Mary, humble servant of the Lord, was open to his every word and call. She was embraced by Francis with indescribable love and declared the protectress and advocate of his family. The Secular Franciscans should express their ardent love for her by imitating her complete self-giving and by praying earnestly and confidently.

-:- -:- -:-

Questions for shared reflection:

(a) What event in Mary's life brings you closer to her as your mother?

(b) Are you more personally comfortable with Mary as *your* mother or as Mother of the Church?

(c) How often do you recite her rosary, or the Franciscan Crown?

NOTES:

7

AS HUMBLE SERVANTS TO EVERYONE

Obedience

To travel on our pilgrim way in imitation of Jesus Christ demands, in the first place, that we are "not to be served, but to serve." This requires submission of our own inclinations in order to fulfill the will of God. This will is made known to us by the directives of those who possess the authority of God, by the circumstances of our state in life, and very often by the needs of others. The foundation of all holiness, of growth in the love of God, is the surrender of our own wills to him.

The Word of God

Your attitude must be that of Christ: Though he was in the form of God, he did not deem equality with God something to be grasped at. Rather, he emptied himself and took the form of a slave, being born in the likeness of men. He was known to be of human estate, and it was thus that he humbled himself, obediently accepting even death, death on a cross.

— *Phillipians 2:5-8*

He went on to address a parable to the guests, noticing how they were trying to get the places of honor at the table: "When you are invited by someone to a wedding party, do not sit in the place of honor in case some greater dignitary has been invited. Then the host might come and say to you, 'Make room for this man,' and you would have to proceed shamefacedly to the lowest place. What you should do when you have been invited is go and sit in the lowest place, so that when your host approaches you he will say, 'My friend, come up higher.' This will win you the esteem of your fellow guests. For everyone who exalts himself shall be humbled and he who humbles himself shall be exalted."

—Luke 14:7:1

Jesus then called them together and said: "You know how those who exercise authority among the Gentiles lord it over them; their great ones make their importance felt. It cannot be like that with you. Anyone among you who aspires to greatness must serve the rest, and whoever wants to rank first among you must serve the needs of all. Such is the case with the Son of Man who has come, not to be served by others, but to serve, to give his own life as a ransom for the many."

—Matthew 20:25-28

Also: Gn 22:1-44 (obedience of Abraham); Lk 1:38 (servant of the Lord); Lk 2:51 (Jesus obeys Mary and Joseph); Jn 4:31-34, 5:30, 6:37-38 (doing the will of his Father; Rm 13:1-7 (obedience to authority); I Pt 2:13-17 (obedience of citizens).

The Church Speaks

Like all Christians, the laity should promptly accept in Christian obedience what is decided by the pastors who, as teachers and rulers of the Church, represent Christ. In this they will follow Christ's example who, by his obedience unto death, opened the blessed way of the liberty of the sons of God to all men.

— Constitution on the Church, 37

By their profession of obedience, religious offer the full dedication of their own wills as a sacrifice of themselves to God, and by this means they are united more permanently and securely with God's saving will. After the example of Jesus Christ, who came to do his Father's will and "taking the form of a servant" (Phil. 2:7) learned obedience through what he suffered, religious moved by the Holy Spirit subject themselves in faith to those who hold God's place, their superiors.

—Decree on the Renewal of Religious Life, 14

Obedience

The priestly ministry, being the ministry of the Church itself, can only be fulfilled in the hierarchical union of the whole body of the Church. Hence pastoral charity urges priests to act within this communion and by obedience to dedicate their own will to the service of God and their fellow Christians.

— *Decree on the Ministry and Life of Priests, 15*

Also: Ch 41, 42; MW 93.

Franciscan Focus

Like Francis, to be obedient because Jesus was obedient! This is all the reason we need. Through the obedience of Jesus to the will of his Father in heaven, we have been redeemed.

Obedience is the practical exercise of faith — belief in the goodness of our Father. Even as he willed the suffering and death of his Son on the cross, he will give us every opportunity to cooperate in that act of our redemption. As Franciscans, our obedience extends to everyone, not just those in authority, and hence we need firm belief that all men and women are children of God, worthy of our service no matter where they are placed in human society.

Franciscans owe the highest obedience and reverence to the Vicar of Christ on earth, to their own bishops, and their own pastors, as to Jesus Christ himself. They promise obedience in a spirit of service to the superiors of the Order, on every level but particularly on the local or community level. This obedience involves everything that pertains to community life in conformity with their responsibilities outside the Order. Above all, they renounce their own wills, leaving all judgment of others to God. By becoming servants to all as Jesus was our servant, they secure their own salvation and, through their obedience, the salvation of all.

Our submission then is to God's will as it is known through his commandments, through his Church, through the needs of those for whom we are responsible, and indeed through whatever need is presnted to us. Our response will be generous if we consider ourselves everybody's servant, as Francis told us we are. Our own judgment of what might be the better way will take second place, and we will not consider the cost to ourselves. Our strength will be in the sure knowledge that this is how God wants it.

Obedience to God must be the special attitude of those who exercise his authority, since they are called to execute God's will as they perceive it. They do not exercise their own will. This is why Francis called the superiors of his Order, *ministers,* because they are called to be the servants of their brothers.

If pride is the basis of all sin, then the submission of one's self to God and all his creatures in obedience is the highest expression of humility.

Our Heritage

Our Lord tells us in the Gospel, "Everyone of you who does not renounce all that he possesses cannot be my disciple" (Luke 14:33). A man takes leave of all that he possesses and loses both his body and his life when he gives himself up completely to obedience in the hands of his superiors.

—*Admonitions of St. Francis, 3. Omnibus, p. 79*

Francis once said to his companion: "Among the other things the kindness of God has generously granted me, it has granted me this grace that I would obey a novice of one hour, if he were given me as my guardian, as carefully as I would obey the oldest and most discreet person. "A subject," he said, "should not consider the man in his superior, but Him for whose sake he is a subject. But the more contemptible is he who rules, so much the more does the humility of him who obeys please."

—*II Celano, 151. Omnibus, p. 484*

The man who is in authority and is regarded as the superior should become the least of all and serve his brothers.

—*Letter to All the Faithful. Omnibus, p. 95*

Also: IC 17 (242); IIC 140-154 (475); Mj I, 5 (638), VI, 1-11 (671); Pr 22 (998), 102-106 (1079); MP 39-75 (1165); Fl I, 3 (1306).

The Secular Franciscan Rule

10. Uniting themselves to the redemptive obedience of Jesus, who placed his will into the Father's hands, let them faithfully fulfill the duties proper to the various circumstances of life. Let them also follow the poor and crucified Christ, witnessing to him even in difficulties and persecutions.

14. Secular Franciscans, together with all people of good will, are called to build a more fraternal and evangelical world so that the kingdom of God may be brought about more effectively. Mindful that anyone "who follows Christ, the perfect man, becomes more of a man himself," let them exercise their responsibilities competently in the Christian spirit of service.

-:- -:- -:-

Questions for shared reflection:

(a) Are people afraid to ask your help with "menial" tasks?

(b) How is the exercise of obedience really an act of faith?

(c) How would you handle a directive in obedience from a minister in the Order or the Church who may be younger, less experienced, and not as educated as you, and whom you judge to be making a mistake?

NOTES:

8

AS SIMPLE PILGRIMS

Poverty

Franciscans travel the world as pilgrims on the way to their Father's heavenly kingdom. Therefore, they consider themselves strangers to this world. They live fully aware that everything they have are gifts from God. Simplicity of life-style and a readiness to share all we possess in a spirit of gratitude become the foundation of our Franciscan life.

The Word of God

Jesus said to his disciples: "I assure you, only with difficulty will a rich man enter into the kingdom of God. I repeat what I said: it is easier for a camel to pass through a needle's eye than for a rich man to enter the kingdom of God." . . . Jesus said to them: ". . . everyone who has given up home, brothers or sisters, father or mother, wife or children or property for my sake will receive many times as much and inherit everlasting life."

—*Matthew 29:23-29*

While they were there the days of her confinement were completed. She gave birth to her first-born son and wrapped him in swaddling clothes and laid him in a manger, because there was no room for them in the place where travelers lodged.

—*Luke 2:6-7*

As they were making their way along, someone said to him, "I will be your follower wherever you go." Jesus said to him, "The foxes have lairs, the birds of the sky have nests, but the Son of Man has nowhere to lay his head."

—*Luke 9:57-59*

Also: Mk 10:17-31 (the danger of riches); Lk 5:8-11 (the call of the disciples); Lk 14:12-35 (the cost of discipleship).

The Church Speaks

Just as Christ carried out the work of redemption in poverty and oppression, so the Church is called to follow the same path if she is to communicate the fruits of salvation to men. Christ Jesus, "though he was by nature God . . . emptied himself, taking the nature of a slave" (Phil. 2:6-7), and "being rich, became poor" (2 Cor. 8:9) for our sake. Likewise, the Church, although she needs human resources to carry out her mission, is not set up to seek earthly glory, but to proclaim, and this by her own example, humility and self-denial. Christ was sent by the Father "to bring good news to the poor . . . to heal the contrite of heart" (Lk. 4:18), "to seek and to save what was lost" (Lk. 19:10). Similarly, the Church encompasses with her love all those who are afflicted by human misery and she recognizes in those who are poor and who suffer, the image of her poor and suffering founder.

—*Constitution on the Church, 8*

Priests are invited to embrace voluntary poverty. By it they become more clearly conformed to Christ and more ready to devote themselves to their sacred ministry. For Christ being rich became poor for our sakes, that through his poverty we might be rich. The apostles by their example gave testimony that the free gift of God was to be given freely. They knew both how to abound and how to suffer need.

—*Decree on the Ministry and Life of Priests, 17*

Also: Ap 14; Ch 48-51; MW 67-72; Rl 13.

Franciscan Focus

The title history gives to St. Francis is "Il Poverello" or "The Little Poor Man." Poverty was so close to his heart as the root of his spirit that in the tradition of chivalry he referred to the "queen of virtues" as his Lady Poverty.

The value of poverty is in this: that it shows forth the

manner of life of the Son of God, who admonished his disciples "to take nothing for their journey" (Mark 6:8). Francis wished to be poor because Christ was poor. This was all the reason he needed.

The followers of the poor Christ must, as he did, identify with the poor, the ordinary people. This they should do especially toward those suffering from any injustice caused by man's avarice, which often separates society into the rich and the poor. It is not sufficient to sympathize with those who have little, but to be one with them in their struggle. We need to assist them by our physical presence and becoming, when possible, one of them. At least we must be ready to share our earthly goods.

Thus a Secular Franciscan's life-style must be simple, so that it threatens no one and shows that we indeed do not consider this earth our final home. So the need is for us to use material goods for their functional value rather than for ostentation and comfortable living.

Since hard work is the lot of the poor, Franciscans must be grateful for opportunities to work as a service to their fellowman in imitation of Jesus Christ who himself was a laborer.

Our example will speak more eloquently than anything we can say about trusting in God's providence. Our life of poverty, i.e., simple living, will be a sign of the trust we have in our Father's goodness.

Our Heritage

Among the supernatural gifts which Francis received from God, the Generous Giver, his love for absolute poverty constituted a special privilege which enabled him to grow in spiritual wealth. . . . From the first moment of his religious life until his death, his sole wealth consisted in a habit, a cord, and a pair of trousers, and he was content with that.

The memory of the poverty felt by Christ and his Mother often reduced him to tears and he called poverty the Queen of the Virtues because it was so evident in the life of the King of Kings and of the Queen, his Mother. When the friars asked him privately what virtue made one dearest to Christ, he replied as if revealing his closest secret, "Believe me, my brothers, poverty is the special way of salvation. It is the source of humility and the root of all perfection and its fruit is manifold, though unseen. This is the treasure hidden in the field in the Gospel to buy which we must sell all — and anything that cannot be sold should be abandoned for love of it.

When speaking about poverty to the friars, Francis often quoted the words of the Gospel, "Foxes have holes, and the birds of the air their resting-places; the Son of Man has nowhere to lay his head" (Mt. 8:20), and he gave orders that the houses they built should be small, like those of the poor. There the friars should live not as if the house belonged to them, but as strangers and pilgrims in a house which was not their own.

—*Major Life VII, 2. Omnibus, p. 681*

When Francis was on a pilgrimage to Rome, he put off his fine garments out of love of poverty, clothed himself with the garments of a certain poor man, and joyfully sat among the poor in the vestibule before the church of St. Peter, where there were many poor, and considering himself one of them, he ate eagerly with them.

—*II Celano 8. Omnibus, p. 368*

Also: Fa (93); IC 8-9 (235). 13-15 (239), 76 (292); IIC 55-93 (410), 189-195 (513); Mj I 6 (639), VII 1-13 (680); MP 2-26 (1127); SC (1549).

The Secular Franciscan Rule

11. Trusting in the Father, Christ chose for himself and his mother a poor and humble life, even though he valued created things attentively and lovingly. Let the Secular Franciscans seek a proper spirit of detachment from temporal goods by simplifying their own material needs. Let them be mindful that according to the gospel they are stewards of the goods received for the benefit of God's children.

Thus, in the spirit of the "the Beatitudes," and as pilgrims and strangers on their way to the home of the Father, they should strive to purify their hearts from every tendency and yearning for possession and power.

15. Let them individually and collectively be in the forefront in promoting justice by the testimony of their human lives and their courageous initiatives. Especially in the field of public life, they should make definite choices in harmony with their faith.

16. Let them esteem work both as a gift and as a sharing in the creation, redemption, and service of the human community.

-:- -:- -:-

Questions for shared reflection:

(a) Are you really poor enough to qualify as a follower of St. Francis?

(b) What wealth do you possess that is not material, and how do you intend to "give it to the poor"?

(c) Since poverty, as the "queen of virtues," must permeate our entire Franciscan life, how do you see poverty in relation to the virtues of humility, justice, and charity?

NOTES:

9

WITH HEARTS PURE AND JOYFUL

Chastity

When our life is centered on God and human love is understood as intrinsic to God's love for us, our energies are directed outside of ourselves. Our spirit knows joy in the wonder of God's goodness. This demands control of the sexual powers that are part of our nature, lest we focus our attention on sensual self-fulfillment. Love — human and divine — must be preserved in its total context. Then the heart is undivided; the heart is pure.

The Word of God

Are you not aware that you are the temple of God, and that the Spirit of God dwells in you? If anyone destroys God's temple, God will destroy him. For the temple of God is holy, and you are that temple.

—*I Corinthians 3:16-17*

"You have heard the commandment, 'You shall not commit adultery.' What I say to you is: anyone who looks lustfully at a woman has already committed adultery with her in his thoughts."

—*Matthew 5:27-28*

We know that Christ, once raised from the dead, will never die again; death has no more power over him. His death was death to sin, once for all; his life is life for God. In the same way, you must consider yourselves dead to sin but alive for God in Christ Jesus.

Do not, therefore, let sin rule your mortal body and make you obey its lusts; no more shall you offer the members of your body to sin as weapons for evil. Rather, offer yourselves to God as men who have come back from the dead to life, and your bodies to God as weapons for justice. Sin will no longer have power over you; you are now under grace, not under the law.

—*Romans 6:9-14*

Husbands, love your wives, as Christ loved the Church. He gave himself up for her to make her holy, purifying her in the bath of water by the power of the word, to present to himself a glorious church, holy and immaculate, without stain or wrinkle or anything of that sort. . . . "For this reason a man shall leave his father and mother, and shall cling to his wife, and the two shall be made into one." This is a great foreshadowing: I mean that it refers to Christ and the Church.

—*Ephesians 5:25-32*

Also: Mt 5:31-32 (divorce); ICr 6:12-20 (sexual immorality); 7:1-40 (advice to married and unmarried); Gl 5:13-26 (true freedom).

The Church Speaks

Married love is an eminently human love because it is an affection between two persons rooted in the will and it embraces the good of the whole person; it can enrich the sentiments of the spirit and their physical expression with a unique dignity and ennoble them as the special elements and signs of the friendship proper to marriage. The Lord, wishing to bestow special gifts of grace and divine love on it, has restored, perfected, and elevated it. A love like that, bringing together the human and divine, leads the partners to a free and mutual giving of self, experienced in tenderness and action, and permeates their whole lives; besides, this love is actually developed and increased by the exercise of it. This is a far cry from mere erotic attraction, which is pursued in selfishness and soon fades away in wretchedness.

—*The Constitution on the Church in the Modern World, 49*

The family is, in a sense, a school for human enrichment. But if it is to achieve the full flowering of its life and mission, the married couple must practice an affectionate sharing of thought and common deliberation as well as eager cooperation as parents in the children's upbringing.

—*The Constitution on the Church in the Modern World, 52*

Chastity "for the sake of the kingdom of heaven" (Mt. 19:22), which religious profess, must be esteemed an exceptional gift of grace. It uniquely frees the heart of man (cf. I Cor. 7:32-35), so that he becomes more fervent in love for God and for all men. For this reason it is a special symbol of heavenly benefits, and for religious it is a most effective means of dedicating themselves wholeheartedly to the divine mission and the works of the apostolate.

—*Decree on Religious Life, 12*

Also: Ap 11, 30; Ch 41; MW 47-52.

Franciscan Focus

To be free to love demands the sacrifice of myself so that God may use me to bring his love to all his people. I cannot love only those I like and find attractive, but I must love everyone without exception, since Christ died for all.

To do this requires a chaste mind and body, since love involves the physical and emotional as well as the spiritual side of man. Without chastity we will find it impossible to love others as children of God. Since "the flesh wars against the spirit," our physical nature seeks its own satisfaction, and must be harnessed so love for God and neighbor can intensify.

An awareness that our sexual nature is particularly vulnerable to selfish responses should make us ever vigilant. However, chastity without charity would be frustrating its purpose. There is lustre to chastity only when it is coupled with a spirit of generosity, peace, and a loving concern for those who are in need.

If we remember only that St. Francis was especially severe on his body in the pursuit of chastity, subjecting it by extreme physical mortification, and forget that this enabled him to love even the most obnoxious leper as he would love Christ, our motivation is misdirected. Above and beyond what is required by God's sixth and ninth commandments, a Franciscan must project by attitude and deportment that our bodies are indeed temples of the Holy Spirit and instruments of service to all people. Marital fidelity, modesty in dress and behavior, and chaste relationships are only the beginning.

As followers of St. Francis we must be leaders within a pagan society to promote respect for the sacredness of sexual love and the dignity of human life from conception to death in all its stages.

Chastity for the single person is perfected by a vow of celibacy, but ordinarily chastity finds its fulfillment in the vows of marriage, where human love flowers, and is sanctified in family life. Strengthened with the sacramental grace of matrimony, married Franciscans reflect the poverty and suffering of Jesus by the joyful way in which they accept the sacrifices necessary to raise a Christian family.

A joyful Christian is a chaste Christian because he is in love with God.

Our Heritage

From the beginning of his conversion to the day of his death, blessed Francis had always been hard on his body. But his primary and main concern was always to possess and preserve spiritual joy within and without. He declared that if a servant of God strove to possess and preserve interior and exterior joy, which proceeds from purity of heart, the devils could do him no harm.

—Legend of Perugia, 97. Omnibus, p. 1073

Francis watched over himself with rigid self-discipline and was especially careful to preserve perfect purity of soul and body. In the early years of his religious life he often jumped into a snow-filled ditch in wintertime, in order to preserve the white robe of purity from the flames of passion and subdue completely the enemy which was part of his own nature.

—Major Life V, 3. Omnibus, p. 664

St. Francis maintained that the safest remedy against the thousand snares and wiles of the enemy is spiritual joy. For he would say: "Then the devil rejoices most when he can snatch away spiritual joy from a servant of God. He carries dust so that he can throw it into even the tiniest chinks of conscience and soil the candor of mind and purity of life. But when spiritual joy fills hearts," he said, "the serpent throws off his deadly poison in vain. The devils cannot harm the servant of Christ when they see he is filled with holy joy. When, however, the soul is wretched, desolate, and filled with sorrow, it is easily overwhelmed by its sorrow or else it turns to vain enjoyments."

—*II Celano 125. Omnibus, p. 465*

Also: Ad (83); Fa (98); IIC 112-118 (454), 204-208 (525).

The Secular Franciscan Rule

12. Witnessing to the good yet to come and obliged to acquire purity of heart because of the vocation they have embraced, they should set themselves free to love God and their brothers and sisters.

17. In their family they should cultivate the Franciscan spirit of peace, fidelity, and respect for life, striving to make of it a sign of a world already renewed in Christ.

By living the grace of matrimony, husbands and wives in particular should bear witness in the world to the love of Christ for his Church. They should joyfully accompany their children on their human and spiritual journey by providing a simple and open Christian education and being attentive to the vocation of each child.

-:- -:- -:-

Questions for shared reflection:

(a) Although chastity directs our total being — physical, emotional, and spiritual — to the perfection of love, what types of persons do you still find it very difficult to forgive or to reach out to with friendship?

(b) Would your friends consider you a joyful person?

(c) Besides your personal example, how are you involved as an individual or as a family in promoting proper attitudes in our sexually-oriented society?

NOTES:

10

AS HERALDS OF THE GREAT KING

Our Apostolic Life

To live the gospel life in its fullness means that we go forth into the world to proclaim the Kingdom of God. Franciscans, as apostles, are messengers sent to deliver faithfully the good news of Jesus Christ by their words and by their example. This we do in the manner of St. Francis of Assisi.

The Word of God

Jesus now called the Twelve together and gave them power and authority to overcome all demons and to cure diseases. He sent them forth to proclaim the reign of God and heal the afflicted.

—*Luke 9:1-2*

After this, the Lord appointed a further seventy-two and sent them in pairs before him to every town and place he intended to visit. He said to them: "The harvest is rich but the workers are few; therefore, ask the harvest-master to send workers to his harvest. Be on your way, and remember: I am sending you as lambs in the midst of wolves."

—*Luke 10:1-3*

"You are the light of the world. A city set on a hill cannot be hidden. Men do not light a lamp and then put it under a bushel basket. They set it on a stand where it gives light to all in the house. In the same way, your light must shine before men so that they may see goodness in your acts and give praise to your heavenly Father."

—*Matthew 5:14-16*

Also: Mt 28:16-20 (commission of the apostles); Mk 1:

16-18 (the call of the first disciples), 6:7-13 (the mission of the Twelve).

The Church Speaks

In the Church there is diversity of ministry but unity of mission. To the apostles and their successors Christ has entrusted the office of teaching, sanctifying, and governing in his name and by his power. But the laity are made to share in the priestly, prophetical, and kingly office of Christ; they have therefore, in the Church and the world, their own assignment in the mission of the whole People of God. In the concrete, their apostolate is exercised when they work at the evangelization and sanctification of men; it is exercised too when they endeavor to have the Gospel spirit permeate and improve the temporal order, going about it in a way that bears clear witness to Christ and helps forward the salvation of men. The characteristic of the lay state being a life led in the midst of the world and of secular affairs, laymen are called by God to make of their apostolate, through the vigor of their Christian spirit, leaven in the world.

—*Decree on the Apostolate of the Laity, 2*

The parish offers an outstanding example of community apostolate, for it gathers into a unity all the human diversities that are found there and inserts them into the universality of the Church. The laity should develop the habit of working in the parish in close union with their priests, of bringing before the ecclesial community their own problems, world problems, and questions regarding man's salvation, to examine them together and solve them by general discussion. According to their abilities the laity ought to cooperate in all the apostolic and missionary enterprises of their ecclesial family.

—*Decree on the Apostolate of the Laity, 10*

Peace cannot be obtained on earth unless the welfare of man is safeguarded and people freely and trustingly share with one another the riches of their minds and their talents. A firm determination to respect the dignity of other men and other peoples along with the deliberate practice of fraternal love are absolutely necessary for the achievement of peace. Accordingly, peace is also the fruit of love, for love goes beyond what justice can endure.

— Constitution on the Church in the Modern World, 78

Also: Bs 17; Ch 30-38; MW 88, 93.

Franciscan Focus

The love of St. Francis for Jesus, especially in response to his death on the cross, prompted Francis to make sure that Christ's sacrifice was not in vain. To be a friend of Jesus called for full cooperation in His mission of salvation. He would love all those for whom Christ died and bring them to the knowledge of Jesus crucified.

As Christians we are called to be apostolic: to consider ourselves sent into the world to bear witness to the Christ-life within us. Our life must show forth our faith in the kingdom of heaven and the unity of all in Christ. This rules out all exploitation of others, all enmity and prejudice, and requires a genuine concern for others in their human needs. It calls for a full participation in the efforts of the Church to develop the Kingdom of God in this world.

As Franciscans we fulfill this vocation according to the example of St. Francis. He considered all creatures, inanimate and animate, as the expression of the wisdom and love of our heavenly Father. He sensed that Jesus Christ, his Son, had sanctified all creation by becoming Man. Above all, Francis believed that Jesus Christ had made all men and women brothers and sisters.

In accord with the manner in which Jesus lived in this world, Francis embraced a life of poverty and penance in simplicity and humility, as the servant of all. He treated all persons whatever their spiritual, physical, or social position — yes, even animals and plants — as brothers and sisters in Christ. He dared call the king of the sky Brother Sun.

The followers of St. Francis, whatever their state of life, are missionaries, sent "to make things happen" for the glory of God. They are called to fulfill Christ's work of bringing salvation to all creation. Above all things they act as instruments of peace in a disordered world, between individuals, between groups, and even between man and nature.

We are on a missionary journey. We can never "settle down." We go where we are sent to proclaim the kingdom of God and penance. Hence, when Secular Franciscans come together as a community, they can properly be called "an assembly of apostles."

Our Heritage

Then the holy lover of complete humility went to the lepers and lived with them, serving them most diligently for God's sake; and washing all foulness from them, he wiped away also the corruption of the ulcers, just as he said in his *Testament:* "When I was in sins, it seemed extremely bitter to me to look at lepers, and the Lord himself led me among them and I practiced mercy with them." . . . While he was still clad in secular garments, he met a leper one day and, made stronger than himself, he kissed him. From then on he began to despise himself more and more, until, by the mercy of the Redeemer, he came to perfect victory over himself. Of other poor, too, while he yet remained in the world and still followed the world, he was the helper, stretching forth a hand of mercy to those who had nothing, and showing compassion to the afflicted.

—I Celano, 17. Omnibus, p. 242

When on a certain day the Gospel was read in that church how the Lord sent his disciples out to preach, the holy man of God, assisting there, understood somewhat the words of the Gospel; after Mass he humbly asked the priest to explain the Gospel to him more fully. When he had set forth for him in order all these things, the holy Francis, hearing that the disciples of Christ should not possess gold or silver or money; nor carry along the way scrip, or wallet, or bread, or a staff; that they should not have shoes, or two tunics; but that they should preach the kingdom of God and penance, immediately cried out exultingly: "This is what I wish, this is what I seek, this is what I long to do with all my heart."

—*I Celano 22. Omnibus, p. 246*

As Francis went through a certain woods singing praises to the Lord in the French language, robbers suddenly rushed out upon him. When they asked him in a ferocious tone who he was, the man of God replied confidently in a loud voice: "I am the herald of the great King. What is that to you?"

—*I Celano 17. Omnibus, p. 242.*

Also: Ad 21 (85); IC 23 (247), 29-31 (252), 80 (296); IIC 9 (369); Mj III 2 (647); 3C 25-29 (915), 58 (941).

The Secular Franciscan Rule

18. Moreover they should respect all creatures, animate and inanimate, which "bear the imprint of the Most High," and they should strive to move from the temptation of exploiting creation to the Franciscan concept of universal kinship.

19. Mindful that they are bearers of peace which must be built up unceasingly, they should seek out ways of unity and fraternal harmony through dialogue, trusting in the presence of the divine seed in everyone and in the transforming power of love and pardon.

Messengers of perfect joy in every circumstance, they should strive to bring joy and hope to others.

Since they are immersed in the resurrection of Christ, which gives true meaning to Sister Death, let them serenely tend toward the ultimate encounter with the Father.

-:- -:- -:-

Questions for shared reflection:

(a) How would you describe your apostolic life at this time?
(b) If confined by sickness, how can you still fulfill the apostolic vocation of a Secular Franciscan?
(c) What have been your experiences as an "instrument of peace" in your family, among friends, in your parish, or on the job?

NOTES:

11

RESPONSIBLE FOR EACH OTHER

Our Fraternity Life

A vocation to be a Secular Franciscan contains within it the call to be part of a community within the Order. Through a community our vocation to the apostolic life is nourished, honed, and supported. Fraternity is an integral element of the Franciscan way of life.

The Word of God

"I do not pray for them alone. I pray also for those who will believe in me through their word, that all be one as you, Father, are in me, and I in you; I pray that they may be (one) in us, that the world may believe that you sent me."

—*John 17:20-21*

May God, the source of all patience and encouragement, enable you to live in perfect harmony with one another according to the spirit of Christ Jesus, so that with one heart and voice you may glorify God, the Father of our Lord Jesus Christ.

—*Romans 15:5-6*

Help carry one another's burdens; in that way you will fulfill the law of Christ.

—*Galatians 6:2*

They devoted themselves to the apostles' instruction and the communal life, to the breaking of bread and the prayers.

—*Acts of the Apostles 2:42*

Also: Mt:31-46 ("the least of my brethren"); Rm 12: 9-21 (fraternal charity); ICr 13:1-13 (excellence of love);

Ph 2:1-4 (united in spirit); 1Pt 4:7-11 (mutual charity).

Franciscan Focus

St. Francis saw his Order as a brotherhood within the community of the Church. We are called to be a sign of the unity that exists between all the baptized as the Body of Christ. We relate as brothers and sisters of the same family, mutually loving, serving and supporting one another in our service to Jesus.

This is why the local fraternity of Secular Franciscans, where this intimacy can exist, is the most important unit of the Order's life. We enter the Order by acceptance into a local fraternity, and we continue in the Order within that fraternity. However, it is possible to be transferred to another. Dismissal from one's fraternity for delinquency, or resignation of membership, is dismissal from the Order. In such case, the obligations of profession remain. Only the competent ecclesiastical superior, in the name of the Church, can grant a dispensation, namely, the minister provincial or his delegate.

From the foundation of community life, where they learn to accept and work with each other's differing personalities and talents, Secular Franciscans reach out to all men and women as gifts of God, as images of his Son. We learn to embrace with joy those who are considered "the least of his brethren," those so often "left out" by society.

A community of Secular Franciscans, because they live apart from one another, come together frequently to develop a close personal and spiritual bond with each other. Once a month is considered a minimum. At such gatherings they share their apostolic commitment as followers of St. Francis through prayer, instruction, dialogue, and personal involvement in each other's needs. All members contribute their energies in cooperation with the Council to make every reunion of the community an experience of growth in the spirit of St. Francis. No one can be passive in community life.

From the level of the local fraternity, the Order builds to a regional fraternity, as a union of local fraternities. This is often called a province. Within a nation or a cultural area, regional fraternities are united as a national fraternity. The many national fraternities form the whole Order, or the international fraternity. The individual Secular Franciscan gives financial support to his local fraternity; each fraternity supports the next higher fraternity.

Not only do local fraternities of the Secular Order function together with each other in united service to the Church, but are involved with the other parts of the Franciscan family to show forth a common charism. To be effective instruments of the spirit of St. Francis we must be a clear sign to the Church of the authentic gospel life, the principle of universal brotherhood, and the abiding mercy of our heavenly Father. Franciscans must be visible in the mainstream of the Church's life, especially on the level of the parish community.

Each fraternity of the Secular Franciscan Order is aided in its spiritual growth as a community by the teaching and counsel of a Franciscan religious, called the Spiritual Assistant, who serves as an instructor of Franciscan spirituality and motivator of Franciscan ideals.

The fraternal relationship of Franciscan friars to their secular brothers and sisters has been fostered from the very beginning. However, the Church has also placed the Secular Order under the ecclesiastical jurisdiction of the First Order of St. Francis and the Third Order Regular (T.O.R.). This latter, the Third Order Regular, was the first of many religious orders founded after the death of St. Francis, in accord with his spirit and rule. The First Order, during the fifteenth and sixteenth centuries, was divided into three parts: the Friars Minor Observants, now simply called Friars Minor (O.F.M.); the Friars Minor Conventual (O.F.M.Conv.); the Friars Minor Capuchin (O.F.M.Cap.).

Ministers Provincial of these four jurisdictions are the only ones who can, with the permission of the ordinary, or local bishop, establish fraternities of the Secular Order. Having done so, they are obliged to provide spiritual assistance. Those fraternities established by the superiors of a particular province are united into a Secular Franciscan province.

Community, then, has many dimensions, from the personal to the structural, from the local level to the world level. It serves as the basis and the strength of the Order as a sign of salvation. It is each one's responsibility to reject any form of isolationism, and to promote Franciscan fraternity.

Our Heritage

Many of the people, both noble and ignoble, cleric and lay, impelled by divine inspiration, began to come to St. Francis, wanting to carry on the battle constantly under his discipline and under his leadership. . . . Truly, upon the foundation of constancy a noble structure of charity arose, in which the living stones, gathered from all parts of the world, were erected into a dwelling place of the Holy Spirit. O with what ardor the new disciples of Christ burned! How great was the love that flourished in the members of this pious society! For whenever they came together anywhere, or met one another along the way, as the custom is, there a shoot of spiritual love sprang up.

—I Celano 37-38. Omnibus, p. 260

St. Francis, exhorting all moreover to charity, admonished them to show to one another affability and the friendliness of family life. "I wish," he said, "that my brothers would show themselves to be children of the same mother."

—II Celano 180. Omnibus, p. 505

Also: IC 42-44 (264); IIC 18-19 (378), 39 (396), 172-177 (500); 3C 57-60 (940).

The Secular Franciscan Rule

20. The Secular Franciscan Order is divided into fraternities of various levels — local, regional, national, and international. Each one has its own moral personality in the Church. These various fraternities are coordinated and united according to the norm of this rule and of the constitutions.

21. On various levels, each fraternity is animated and

guided by a council and minister (or president) who are elected by the professed according to the constitutions.

Their service, which lasts for a definite period, is marked by a ready and willing spirit and is a duty of responsibility to each member and to the community.

Within themselves the fraternities are structured in different ways according to the norm of the constitutions, according to the various needs of their members and their regions, and under the guidance of their respective council.

23. Members who find themselves in particular difficulties should discuss their problems with the council in fraternal dialogue. Withdrawal or permanent dismissal from the Order, if necessary, is an act of the fraternity council according to the norm of the constitutions.

24. To foster communion among members, the council should organize regular and frequent meetings of the community as well as meeting with other groups, especially with youth groups. It should adopt appropriate means for growth in Franciscan and ecclesial life and encourage everyone to a life of fraternity. This communion continues with deceased brothers and sisters through prayer for them.

25. Regarding expenses necessary for the life of the fraternity and the needs of worship, of the apostolate, and of charity, all the brothers and sisters should offer a contribution according to their means. Local fraternities should contribute toward the expenses of the higher fraternity councils.

26. As a concrete sign of communion and coresponsibility, the councils on various levels, in keeping with the constitutions, shall ask for suitable and well prepared religious for spiritual assistance. They should make this request to the superiors of the four religious Franciscan families, to whom the Secular Fraternity has been united for centuries.

To promote fidelity to the charism as well as observance of the rule and to receive greater support in the life of the fraternity, the minister or president, with the consent of the council, should take care to ask for a regular pastoral visit by the competent religious superiors as well as for a fraternal visit from those of the higher fraternities, according to the norm of the constitutions.

-:- -:- -:-

Questions for shared reflection:

(a) What contributions have you been able to make to develop the spirit of "family" in your community?

(b) Has your experience with Franciscan community measured up to your expectations? Anything missing?

(c) To what extent have you become familiar with the apostolic work being done by your brothers and sisters in the community?

NOTES:

12

NEVER LOOKING BACK

Profession of the Rule

Our Franciscan pilgrimage, a journey to everywhere with Jesus and Francis, is not ended until death. When our Profession of the Rule is accepted by the Church, there is no turning back to our starting point, nor can we separate ourselves from the company of our brothers and sisters in St. Francis. Having professed to observe the Secular Franciscan Rule, we have made a permanent commitment.

The Word of God

To another he said, "Come after me." The man replied, "Let me bury my father first." Jesus said to him, "Let the dead bury their dead; come away and proclaim the kingdom of God." Yet another said to him, "I will be your follower, Lord, but first let me take leave of my people at home." Jesus answered him, "Whoever puts his hand to the plow but keeps looking back is unfit for the reign of God."

—*Luke 9:59-62*

As your fellow workers we beg you not to receive the grace of God in vain. For he says, "In an acceptable time I have heard you; on a day of salvation I have helped you." Now is the acceptable time! Now is the day of salvation! We avoid giving anyone offense, so that our ministry may not be blamed. On the contrary, in all that we do we strive to present ourselves as ministers of God, acting with patient endurance amid trials, difficulties, distresses, beatings, imprisonments and riots; as men familiar with hard work, sleepless nights, and fasting; conducting ourselves with innocence, knowledge, and patience, in the Holy Spirit, in sincere love as men with the message of truth and the power of God; wielding the weapons of righteousness with right hand and left, whether honored or dishonored, spoken of well or ill. We are called imposters, yet we are truthful; nobodies who in fact are well known; dead, yet here we are alive; punished, but not put to death; sorrowful, though we are always rejoicing; poor, yet we enrich many. We seem to have nothing, yet everything is ours!

—*Corinthians 6:1-10*

Franciscan Focus

Although St. Francis occasionally returned to Assisi after the year 1209, and eventually came back to die there, he spent most of his later years in arduous travel into all parts of Italy and beyond. He sent his friars into every place, remembering the words of Jesus: "Go into the whole world and proclaim the good news to all creation" (Mark 16:15). Hence, Secular Franciscans do not remain in Assisi to enjoy its spiritual consolations. We have been sent by Christ "before him to every town and place he intended to visit" (Luke 10:1), and so we leave Assisi and set out on Our Journey to Everywhere.

The journey beyond Assisi, however, does not begin until one is fully a member of the Order. This happens upon acceptance by the Church of a Profession of the Rule, the promise to live as a Secular Franciscan for the remainder of one's life. Thus the Secular Franciscan is truly *sent by Christ* to proclaim the good news of Jesus Christ.

A candidate or novice may request to make Profession of the Rule upon completion of the period of probation of not less than one year. The council of the fraternity judges when and if the candidate or novice shall be allowed to make profession. The candidate or novice may be accepted, the time of formation may be extended, or be advised that he/she has no vocation to be a Secular Franciscan. When he/she is accepted for profession, the fraternity minister requests the Spiritual Assistant to receive the profession. In the name of the Church, he makes his own determination of the candidate's fitness. He may accede to the council's request, deny it, or extend the formation period.

Profession is a personal response, freely given under the inspiration of grace, to God's call to follow in the footsteps of his Son according to the way of St. Francis of Assisi. Made before a legitimate superior, delegated to represent the Church, it is a solemn public religious act by which one commits his/her life to God in the Secular Franciscan Order. We promise to observe the commandments of God and the holy Gospel of our Lord Jesus Christ according to the example of St. Francis. Profession takes place with full solemnity during the Sacrifice of the Mass in the presence of the fraternity.

Since Profession of the Rule is not an act of private devotion, but is accepted in the name of the Church, it is binding until death. Only the Church can grant a release from the obligations incurred by profession.

Profession in the Secular Franciscan Order is not the taking of vows; it is not a promise binding under pain of sin. It is a re-affirmation of one's baptismal promises, to live more fully the Christian life by a commitment of service within an Order and according to a way of life approved by the Church. Hence, the response made to the newly professed during the profession ceremony takes on great significance: "If you observe what you have promised, I, on the part of Almighty God, promise you life everlasting."

Our Heritage

But, though the glorious father had been brought to the fullness of grace before God and shone among men of this world by his good works, he nevertheless thought always to begin more perfect works. . . . For true virtue knows not a limit of time, since the expectation of a reward is eternal. Therefore he was afire with a very great desire to return to the first beginnings of humility and, by reason of the immensity of his love, rejoicing in hope, he thought to recall his body to its former subjection, even though it had already come to such an extremity. . . . Though he found it necessary to moderate his early rigor because of his infirmity, he would still say: "Let us begin, brothers, to serve the Lord God, for up to now we have made little or no progress."

—*I Celano, 103. Omnibus, p. 317*

As the moment of his death drew near, the saint . . . added, "I bid you goodbye, all you my sons, in the fear of God. Remain in him always. There will be trials and temptations in the future, and it is well for those who persevere in the life they have undertaken. I am on my way to God, and I commend you all to this favor."

—*Major Life XIV, 5. Omnibus, p. 740*

Also: IIC 32-34 (390).

The Secular Franciscan Rule

23. Profession by its nature is a permanent commitment.

Epilogue of the Rule

Blessing of St. Francis from the *Testament*.

"May whoever observes all this be filled in heaven with the blessing of the most high Father, and on earth with that of his beloved Son, together with the Holy Spirit, the Comforter."

-:- -:- -:-

Questions for shared reflection:

(a) Do you feel adequately prepared for a life-long commitment as a Secular Franciscan?

(b) What apprehension do you feel about making Profession of the Rule?

(c) Are you ready to request the Fraternity minister to be allowed to make Profession?

NOTES: